Access, Diversity, Equity, and Inclusion in Cultural Organizations

Analyzing the lack of diversity among opera executives, this book examines the careers of executive opera managers of color in the U.S. By interrogating the impact of race on arts managers' careers, the author contemplates how opera might attract and retain more racially diverse arts managers to ensure its future.

With a focus on the U.S., research is contextualized via qualitative data to explore, enhance, and institutionalize access, diversity, equity, and inclusion (ADEI) in the opera industry. In a revealing series of expert-conducted interviews, the author poses illuminating questions, such as:

- what if an inability to recruit and retain diverse executives is the primary source of opera's challenges?
- if more racially diverse opera executives existed, would the art form persist in struggling to find its place in contemporary society?
- from where will the next generation of diverse opera managers emerge?

As the magnitude of the global diversity problem grows within the creative and cultural industries, this book serves as a guide for Arts Management practitioners and students who may view their class, different ability, ethnicity, gender, race, or sexual orientation as a liability in their pursuit of executive careers.

Antonio C. Cuyler, Ph.D. is Director of the MA Program and Associate Professor of Arts Administration at Florida State University, USA.

Routledge Research in the Creative and Cultural Industries
Series Editor: Ruth Rentschler

This series brings together book-length original research in cultural and creative industries from a range of perspectives. Charting developments in contemporary cultural and creative industries thinking around the world, the series aims to shape the research agenda to reflect the expanding significance of the creative sector in a globalised world.

Published titles in this series include:

Building Better Arts Facilities
Lessons from a U.S. National Study
Joanna Woronkowicz, D. Carroll Joynes & Norman Bradburn

Rethinking Strategy for Creative Industries
Innovation and Interaction
Milan Todorovic

Arts Governance
People, Passion, Performance
Ruth Rentschler

Artistic Interventions in Organizations
Research, Theory and Practice
Edited by Ulla Johansson Sköldberg, Jill Woodilla & Ariane Berthoin Antal

The Classical Music Industry
Chris Dromey & Julia Haferkorn

Arts and Business
Building a Common Ground for Understanding Society, 1st Edition
Edited by Elena Raviola & Peter Zackariasson

Performing Arts Center Management
Edited by Patricia Dewey Lambert & Robyn Williams

Arts and Cultural Management
Sense and Sensibilities in the State of the Field
Edited by Constance DeVereaux

Managing Organisational Success in the Arts
Edited by David Stevenson

Music Business Careers
Career Duality in the Creative Industries
Cheryl Slay Carr

Racial and Ethnic Diversity in the Performing Arts Workforce
Tobie S. Stein

Understanding Audience Engagement in the Contemporary Arts
Stephanie E. Pitts, Sarah M. Price

Access, Diversity, Equity, and Inclusion in Cultural Organizations
Insights from the Careers of Executive Opera Managers of Color in the U.S.
Antonio C. Cuyler

Access, Diversity, Equity, and Inclusion in Cultural Organizations

Insights from the Careers of Executive Opera Managers of Color in the U.S.

Antonio C. Cuyler, Ph.D.

Routledge
Taylor & Francis Group

LONDON AND NEW YORK

First published 2021
by Routledge
2 Park Square, Milton Park, Abingdon, Oxon OX14 4RN

and by Routledge
605 Third Avenue, New York, NY 10017

First issued in paperback 2022

Routledge is an imprint of the Taylor & Francis Group, an informa business

Publisher's Note
The publisher has gone to great lengths to ensure the quality of this
reprint but points out that some imperfections in the original copies
may be apparent.

British Library Cataloguing in Publication Data
A catalogue record for this book is available from the British Library

Library of Congress Cataloging-in-Publication Data
A catalog record has been requested for this book

ISBN 13: 978-0-367-55788-1 (pbk)
ISBN 13: 978-1-138-58710-6 (hbk)
ISBN 13: 978-0-429-50417-4 (ebk)

DOI: 10.4324/9780429504174

Typeset in Sabon
by Taylor & Francis Books

For Alyssa & Collin

Contents

Tables

Acknowledgements

This book is the result of 13 years of in-depth study of the careers of executive opera managers of color in the U.S. without whom I would not have completed this book. My deepest appreciation to Henry Akina, Torrie Allen, Wayne Brown, Michael Ching, Linda Jackson, and Willie Anthony Waters for the generosity of your time. Your careers, lived experiences, and managerial perspectives continue to fascinate me. I owe gratitude to the Florida State University (FSU) Council on Research and Creativity for providing me summer salary support through its Committee on Faculty Research Support (COFRS) program to work on this book during the summer of 2019. To colleagues: Karen Chandler, Brea Heidelberg, Morenga Hunt, Keith Lee, Tobie Stein, Jason White, and Mark Banks, thank you for creating work that has inspired me. To Routledge, thank you for your patience and support throughout the writing process. Lastly, to my students of color, thank you for your courage to envision careers in the arts that place you in leadership roles so that those whom the cultural sector has consciously and unconsciously disenfranchised will receive their creative justice.

1 Overture: Introduction

In the U.S., opera generates more than \$1 billion in revenue, and employs nearly 35,000 people annually. Yet, despite size, personnel expenses range from 60–70% of opera companies' budgets, and ticket revenue covers less than 40% of core artistic expenses (OPERA America, 2020a; and OPERA America, 2020b). Contributions supplement the majority of opera companies' budgets. In addition, since 2014, the percentage of core programs covered by earned revenue has continuously trended downward (OPERA America, 2020a). Furthermore, according to the National Endowment for the Arts (2019), in 2017 only 2% of U.S. adults reported attending an opera during the last 12 months, and the average number of times that they reported attending an opera decreased from two in 2012 to 1.5 in 2017. Low ticket sales, an aging audience, a shrinking donor base, rising costs, boards with reductionist thinking, and an apathetic society suggest that opera in the U.S. exist in an endless state of crisis; so much so that Rivera (2017) perceptively raised the question, "is opera circling the toilet?"

The enduring lack of racial diversity in opera, particularly among opera managers, is most disheartening to me, especially since the U.S. Census Bureau has warned of impending demographic shifts to a minority–majority society by the year 2045 (Fey, 2018). One might consider this problem unique to the U.S.; however, because Australia, Canada, France, and the UK have racial demographics similar to the U.S., the "diversity problem" has become increasingly internationalized and will become more so as more immigrants of color migrate to historically racially homogenous countries such as Denmark, Finland, Iceland, Norway, and Sweden. Though the opera industry should view this problem cross-culturally, holistically, and interculturally (Henze, 2018; and Henze & Wolfram, 2014); what if opera's inability to recruit and retain racially diverse opera managers, including executives, is the primary source of all of its challenges?

In 2001, cultural economists Heilbrun and Gray asserted that to survive, art forms with Western European origins such as ballet, opera, and symphonic music needed to diversify their audiences. This imperative raised several questions for me. First, would more racially diverse opera managers and executives attract more racially diverse audiences? Second, if more racially diverse opera managers and executives existed, would the art form continue to struggle to find its place in the 21st century? Third, and perhaps most important, if opera truly cares about access, diversity, equity, and inclusion (ADEI), from where might it recruit the next generation of racially diverse opera managers and executives?

Though this book does not explicitly address these questions, it aims to help the opera industry begin to honestly grapple with these questions for its sustainability in and beyond the 21st century. By examining the careers of executive opera managers of color in the U.S., this book also: (1) explores the impact of race on the careers of executive opera managers of color in the U.S., (2) identifies beneficial experiences to their careers, (3) describes factors that advanced or served as barriers to their careers, (4) identifies career strategies, (5) contemplates how opera might attract and retain more racially diverse managers, and lastly (6) serves as inspiration for Arts Management professionals and students around the globe who may view their class, different ability, ethnicity, gender, race, or sexual orientation as a liability in their pursuit of executive-level management careers in Arts Management.

My positionality

I was born and grew up mostly in Winter Haven, Florida. My introduction to opera came by way of my childhood church's adult choir. The choir director sang gospel with an operatically infused voice. That sound has stayed with me even to this day. My next significant interaction with opera came via a 1993 *Time Magazine* issue that featured Marian Anderson on the cover after she died. I have no clue how or why this issue appeared in my household, but it inspired me to think differently about the professional possibilities in the arts available to Black Americans living in the U.S.

Growing up Black American and working class, one might assume that opera would not have such an impact on my life. But, opera greatly impacted me. For high school, I attended the Lois Cowles Harrison Visual and Performing Arts Center where I became the first Black male to graduate from the Voice program. Harrison allowed me to discover a passion for opera that inspired me to frequently visit public libraries in both Winter Haven and Lakeland, Florida to consume as much opera as

I could through books, recordings, and videos. I am certain that my interest in opera distracted me and kept me out of trouble. By the time I arrived at Stetson University as an 18-year-old undergraduate, I had a superb education in music that prepared me very well to thrive in my degree program in Voice and Foreign Languages. After Stetson, I earned a Master's of Arts in Arts Administration, as well as a Ph.D. in Art Education with a major in Arts Administration from the Florida State University (FSU). Though I value the education I received immensely, I fully acknowledge that race impacted my music education.

In hindsight, my music education was very much an enculturation and socialization process, colonialist and imperialist even at times. For example, most of my White voice teachers discouraged me from singing gospel, stating, "Antonio, if you want to become a serious opera singer, you're going to have to stop singing gospel." To some, this instruction may seem accurate and appropriate. But for me, it created an artistic existential crisis because gospel served as the vehicle by which I first discovered my singing voice. Comparatively, my choir directors at church never once discouraged me from singing or studying opera. Perhaps they saw studying opera as a way to enhance my gospel singing.

As I ponder what opera might have gained from me severing my ties to gospel and all Black music idioms, today, I cannot help but to consider that particular instruction that I received racist. As a descendent of African slaves from Angola, Guinea Bissau, Liberia, Senegal, and Sierra Leone born in the U.S., I have a great deal of experience with racism. In fact, as a Black American, I have had difficulty identifying even one aspect of my life that racism has not impacted in some way. Indeed, as Critical Race Theorists have argued, structural and systemic racism has led to a great deal of racialized suffering visited upon Black, Indigenous, People of Color (BIPOC). Racism has also led to White people receiving unearned privilege simply because of their race (Crenshaw et al., 1996; and McIntosh, 1989). This very reason explains why a White voice teacher would feel emboldened to instruct me to discontinue singing music critically important to my understanding of who I am. Nevertheless, I consider the internalized racism I had to fight against as a result of this seemingly harmless instruction more ominous.

According to Bivens (2005), as people of color experience racism, they internalize it and develop actions, behaviors, beliefs, and ideas that support or collude with racism. I agree with Bivens (2005) that internalized racism has its own systemic reality and negative consequences that impact how BIPOC live their lives and see themselves. Clearly, just as a system exists that reinforces the power and expands the privilege of White people, a system also exists to actively discourage and undermine the power of BIPOC. Had I listened to my voice teachers, internalized racism would have caused me to lose a firm understanding of who I am ancestrally, artistically, creatively, culturally, historically, psychologically, socially, and spiritually. This key racialized self-understanding could only come from gospel, and other Black music idioms. But, internalized racism is one of the most vile ways that race and racism intertwines the fates of BIPOC and White people in a hellish cycle of imprisonment.

Whereas BIPOC have to battle the effects of internalized racism, I argue that the sifecta of White fragility (DiAngelo, 2018), White guilt (Steele, 2007), White privilege (McIntosh, 1989), White rage (Anderson, 2017), White savior industrial complex (Bex & Craps, 2016; Straubhaar, 2015; and Yusuf, 2016), and White supremacy (LeRoy, 2018; and PBS, 2017) makes it exceedingly difficult for most White people to acknowledge their part in racism. Indeed, the moment that a White person learns of their privilege it can lead some down the path of fragility and rage, while others take the path of guilt and the savior complex. In addition, while BIPOC can share the impact of racism on their lived experiences to possibly compel change, White people should not ask or expect them to do the exhausting emotional and intellectual labor of helping them to become anti-racist. White accomplices and allies who "get it" should bear this responsibility. I share these specific aspects of my lived experiences and views so that readers will understand the unique perspective I bring to this book. Living as a Black American who is also very well educated in the arts, and in particular opera, is the positionality I use to examine the managerial aspects of the art form critically and meaningfully from a place of tremendous love.

A bit of U.S. operatic history

U.S. operatic history began in February of 1735 in Charleston, South Carolina with a performance of the ballad opera, *Flora* or *Hob in the Well* (Dizikes, 1993). At that time, Puritanism posed a threat to opera's evolution in the U.S. In fact, few expected that the art form would become popular. Immigration, politics, war, and events in Europe also affected U.S. operatic history. Nevertheless, Dizikes (1993) argued that the first critical notice of the opera, *Love in a Village* by Thomas Arne, served as an indication of a maturing operatic culture in the U.S. After then, opera played a much larger part in the theatrical repertory offered by touring companies, making it a livelier element of popular culture.

Between the end of the 1760s and 1883, New Orleans' thriving arts culture influenced the evolution of opera in the U.S. Between 1803 and

1815, opera troupes in New Orleans gave over 700 performances of 150 different operas by 50 composers. Furthermore, between 1827 and 1833, New Orleans provided northern cities with almost all of the European opera they heard (Crawford, 2001; and Dizikes, 1993). In New Orleans, opera also demonstrated its ability to attract a racially diverse audience. Members of the entire population made up audiences, including slaves of African descent though laws restricted them to the gallery. Dizikes (1993) maintained that New Orleans' early operatic history illustrated the central importance of the audience for opera in the U.S. This highlighted opera's need to compete within the U.S. capitalist entertainment market for its audience because governments had not yet established the sophisticated cultural public funding systems that exist today (Rushton, 2018; and Siefert, 2004).

In 1998, Cheatham argued that the newly rich had a considerable impact on the history of opera in the U.S., particularly in the northeastern region of the country. The establishment of the Metropolitan Opera in October 1883, for example, supports his assertion. A handful of New York's wealthiest families formed the now infamous Metropolitan Opera for their social benefit and pleasure. As time progressed, the Metropolitan Opera grew beyond the vanities of its original benefactors, and now more than 130 million people benefit annually in person or through live streaming from the creative and artistic genius of the world's finest opera house (Cheatham, 1998; and Dizikes, 1993).

Rudolph Bing's (1902–97) arrival as General Manager at the Metropolitan proved one of the most exciting times in its history. Bing achieved a great deal during his tenure. To name two key successes, he lengthened the New York season from 18 to 31 weeks and restructured the subscription season by offering shorter series that quadrupled the number of subscribers from 5,000 to 21,000. Yet, in my view, his position on civil rights remains his most notable achievement. He broke the racial barrier by engaging the ballerina, Janet Collins, as the first Black American artist to appear on the Met's stage (Bing, 1972; Cheatham, 1997; Dizikes, 1993; and Fiedler, 2001). In addition, during Bing's management an increase of Black opera singers appeared at the Met. This list includes luminaries such as Marian Anderson and Robert McFerrin, the first Black American female and male to sing lead roles. Leontyne Price, George Shirley, Martina Arroyo, Grace Bumbry, Shirley Verrett, Seth McCoy, and Simon Estes also made their Metropolitan operatic debuts during Bing's tenure. After Bing, James Levine continued similar casting policies that added a number of gifted Black opera singers to the Met's roster, too, including Kathleen Battle, Vinson Cole, Barbara Hendricks, Leona Mitchell, Jessye Norman, and Willard White (Cheatham, 1997; Fiedler, 2001; and Story, 1990).

Between 1982 and 1992, the U.S. opera audience grew by 35%. This trend continued through 2002 when the opera audience grew by an additional 8.2% (National Endowment for the Arts, 2002). This is by and large due to the development of regional opera companies. In fact, according to OPERA America (2020b), 88% of the 50 largest U.S. cities have professional opera companies. I argue that the Met's national tours and Saturday afternoon broadcasts inspired the proliferation of regional opera companies that emerged between 1965 and 1980. Yet, today, opera remains one of the most unattended of all performing art forms in the U.S. Several reasons may explain a lack of nonattendance including perceptions of elitism, a lack of access to opera education, ticket prices, competition with other entertainment options, among others, including the risk-adverse nature of opera companies.

Indeed, risk-aversion causes opera managers to program the "tried and proven" over the "new and risky." Operas that managers program impact their ability to attract, develop, and retain larger and more racially diverse audiences. For example, during the 2018–19 season, the list of the five most produced operas included Puccini's *La Bohème*, Verdi's *La Traviata*, Bizet's *Carmen*, Rossini's *Il Barbiere di Siviglia*, and Puccini's *Madama Butterfly*. This list favors the creative contributions to opera made by dead, European, heterosexual, temporarily abled-bodied, and cisgender men. Even when producing more contemporary North American operas and despite the fact that a woman composed one of the operas on the list, managers solely programmed works by White composers including Heggie's *Three Decembers*, Kaminsky's *As One*, Bernstein's *West Side Story* & *Candide*, and Puts' *Silent Night*. Though opera composers of color such as Armienta, Blanchard, Ching, Davis, and Joplin, among others, exist and have existed, only this year did the Metropolitan Opera plan to stage its first opera written by a Black American composer (Cooper, 2019; and Walls, 2019). However, due to COVID-19, the MET has suspended all performances.

Though I mentioned it earlier when acknowledging that slaves of African descent attended operas in New Orleans, one cannot underestimate the enduring impacts of 346 years of slavery, Jim Crow laws, and segregation pre-Civil Rights on if, how, why, and when BIPOC, attend or participate in opera in the U.S., or not (André, 2018; Cheatham, 1998, 1997; Smith, 1995; and Story, 1990). Clearly, the opera industry must exhaust its cultural, financial, intellectual, political, and social capital to ensure that all people can live creative and expressive lives on their own terms through opera (Cuyler, 2019). The opera industry could do this by creating more entry points into opera for all people despite their differences. Still, prejudice, perceived or real, against opera presents an obstacle to attendance and participation that the opera industry must address before its audiences, boards, programming, and staffs can become more racially diverse and more accurately reflect the racial demographics of U.S. society. Given its leadership, vast social network, and resources, perhaps OPERA America, the service arts organization for opera in the U.S., can lead this transformation.

OPERA America

Founded in 1970 as the only service arts organization for opera in the U.S., OPERA America's mission endeavors to support the creation, presentation, and enjoyment of opera (OPERA America, 2020c). The year 2020 marked the 50th anniversary of the service arts organization's existence. Currently, OPERA America has an international membership that includes 510 business members, 1,700 individual members, 80,000 visitors to the National Opera Center, 750 opera conference attendees, 50,000 social media followers, and 18,000 email subscribers (OPERA America, 2020b). According to a field report given by the President and CEO of OPERA America, Marc Scorca, in 2019 opera companies sold more than 2.5 million tickets across 300+ venues and awarded 112 grants to companies and creators.

Structurally, OPERA America organizes its opera company members according to five budget sizes. Budget 1 ($15 million+) includes opera companies such as Houston Grand Opera, Los Angeles Opera, Lyric Opera of Chicago, Opera Philadelphia, San Francisco Opera, Santa Fe Opera, and Seattle Opera. Among the Budget 2 ($3 million to $15 million) companies includes the Atlanta Opera, Dallas Opera, and Michigan Opera Theatre, to name a few. Opera companies such as the Hawaii Opera Theatre and Opera Memphis fit into the Budget 3 category ($1 million to $3 million). Budget 4 ($250,000 to $1 million) companies include Anchorage Opera, Opera Birmingham, and Opera for the Young, among others. Lastly, Budget 5 ($250,000 and under) companies include American Lyric Theater, Chelsea Opera, the Cleveland Opera, and Solo Opera, among others. As the budget size of companies relates to executive opera managers of color, the executives in this book have only worked at a level 2 company (Wayne Brown, Michigan Opera Theatre), level 3 company (Henry Akina, Hawaii Opera Theatre, Michael Ching, Opera Memphis, Linda Jackson and Willie Anthony Waters, Connecticut Opera before it closed), and level 4 company (Torrie Allen, Anchorage Opera). To date, not one BIPOC opera exectuive has managed at a level 1 company, or the Metropolitan

Opera, whose $300 million+ budget is so large that OPERA America categorizes it separately.

Access, diversity, equity, and inclusion (ADEI)

In 2011, Sidford re-invigorated longstanding discourses about racial ADEI when she reported that the majority of arts funding supports large organizations with budgets greater than $5 million that primarily present Western European arts forms and serve White audiences. With this realization, many service arts organizations initiated conversations about cultural equity and developed initiatives to try and address ADEI issues related to ability, class, ethnicity, gender, race, and sexual orientation. Though the topic of diversity served as the focus of the 2005 OPERA America annual conference in Detroit, Michigan, and the highly regarded principal consultant of artEquity, Carmen Morgan, designed customized resources for OPERA America, one could describe the service arts organization's response at that time to Sidford's work as tepid. Six years later, in 2017, Helicon Collaborative, Sidford's consulting firm, reported that despite a greater awareness of the problem, the distribution of arts funding became less equitable.

This suggests that legacy cultural organizations, such as opera companies, privileged by the inequitable cultural funding system, doubled down on their efforts to preserve and protect the share of the funding to which they have always felt entitled. Sidford's (2011; and Helicon Collaborative, 2017) findings informed the U.S. cultural sector of known truths about racial ADEI issues relative to funding. It also disrupted well-established norms and promised to inspire seismic paradigmatic shifts. However, from the outside looking in, OPERA America appeared slow to respond to these shifts in comparison to the service arts organizations for dance, museums, symphony, and theatre.

In fact, when conducting a study on bullshitting in service arts organizations' ADEI statements, by November 2018, all but OPERA America had developed an ADEI statement. Most service arts organizations also provided resources to their members for how to manage the implementation of ADEI. In and of itself, not having such a statement does not suggest that OPERA America did not care about ADEI issues. In fact, one could argue that responding more slowly may have given OPERA America a strategic advantage to assess all of the approaches their colleagues used to determine the best way forward for its members and the opera industry as a whole. Conversely, one could also ask, did OPERA America lose momentum for addressing ADEI issues in the opera industry by waiting too long? Nevertheless, when the service arts organization finally responded it did so with a seemingly comprehensive and well-thought-out approach for addressing ADEI in the opera industry that I will critically examine in Chapter 8 of this book.

Why this book now?

I began collecting data for my dissertation on the careers of non-European executive opera administrators in the U.S. in May of 2006. At that time, only four executive opera managers of color existed in the U.S. Michael Ching, Linda Jackson, and Willie Anthony Waters all participated in my study. Henry Akina declined to participate in the study at that time. Although the study made a valuable contribution to the literature, more than ten years later fewer executive opera managers of color exist in the U.S. in 2020 than in 2007. In addition, after collecting data for the study, Torrie Allen assumed executive leadership of Anchorage Opera from 2006–2012, and Wayne Brown assumed the role of President and CEO at Michigan Opera Theatre in 2014.

Second, over the last 30 years cultural critics and scholars have given the topic of race in opera considerable attention as it relates to characters, composers, librettos, and singers (André, 2018; André, Bryan, & Saylor, 2012; Caplan, 2017; Cheatham, 1998; 1997; Garre-Schmidt, 2000; Hu, 2019; Midgette, 2019; Smith, 1995; and Story, 1990). Furthermore, Arts Management scholars have examined aspects of opera management including artistic dichotomies (Auvinen, 2001), audience development and evaluation (Agostino, 2018), cultural policy (Rushton, 2018; Siefert, 2004), funding (Mayer, 1987), management of Italian opera houses (Sicca, 1997), management of the Met (Volpe, 2006), and management of the New York City Opera (Waleson, 2018). Only Stein (2000; and 2020) has explicitly advocated for the need to create more opportunities for people of color in Performing Arts Management. To date, only my previously mentioned work has also done so specifically for opera managers (Cuyler, 2007). Yet, some Arts Management students of color aspire to pursue careers in opera management.

Third, in my more than ten years as an Arts Management educator I have taught BIPOC and White students who have sought careers in opera management after graduation. By following their careers closely, I have observed that my White students, who also identified as cisgender male and gay, have achieved considerable success. However, my BIPOC students have struggled to secure careers in opera management. In my observations of these two populations, both the White and BIPOC students had equal passion and knowledge of the art form. They also had a solid education that prepared them well to thrive in the opera industry. But, why have the BIPOC students had markedly different experiences pursuing careers in opera management?

Does the opera industry have unconscious racial biases that may make it difficult for BIPOC to navigate successful careers in opera management even when they are reasonably prepared professionally? If so, is the opera industry truly ready to do the work necessary to adopt and institutionalize practices that will support and ensure the success of its racial ADEI efforts, and open doors for more racially diverse opera managers? In addition, if the opera industry has unconscious racial bias, by what means might the opera industry recognize and address its unconscious racial bias to empower the cultural capital of BIPOC to attract, develop, and retain a more racially diverse network of people who participate in opera?

Summary

To date, no book has investigated the careers of racially diverse executives in opera in depth to identify the factors that advanced or impeded their careers, or the strategies they used to break through the glass ceiling in Arts Management. This book uses longitudinal qualitative data to build upon previous research by further investigating the careers of executive opera managers of color in the U.S. In addition to the previously conducted interviews with Michael Ching, Linda Jackson, and Willie Anthony Waters, interviews with Henry Akina, Torrie Allen, and Wayne Brown served as data in this book to comprehensively present the careers of the only six known people of color to manage major opera companies in the U.S. at the executive level. By executive level, I mean BIPOC who have held the position of Artistic Director, Executive Director, General Director, General Manager, or President & CEO at major opera companies.

This book includes eight chapters organized into eight acts. Act II–VII includes Chapters 2–7; I have dedicated a chapter to each opera manager of color in this study. I organized each opera manager's chapter according to Super's (1953; and 1957) vocational choice theory which details how one's career development progresses over their lifespan. These stages of development include: growth (age 0–14), exploration (age 15–24), establishment (age 25–44), maintenance (age 45–64), and decline (age 65+). Act VIII, the final act, includes Chapter 8 wherein I discuss experiences beneficial to the careers of BIPOC executive opera managers of color in the U.S., factors that advanced or served as barriers to their careers, and career strategies. I also contemplate how opera might attract and retain more racially diverse managers, as well as possibilities that opera might explore to enhance and further institutionalize ADEI to transform the opera industry.

References

Agostino, D. (2018). Can Twitter add to performance evaluation in the area of performing arts? Reflections from La Scala Opera House. *Journal of Arts Management, Law, and Society*, 48(5), 321–338.

Anderson, C. (2017). *White rage: The unspoken truth of our racial divide*. Bloomsbury.

André, N. (2018). *Black opera: History, power, engagement*. University of Illinois Press.

André, N., Bryan, K. M., & Saylor, E. (2012). *Blackness in opera*. University of Illinois Press.

Auvinen, T. (2001). Why is it difficult to manage an opera house? The artistic-economic dichotomy and its manifestations in the organizational structures of five opera organizations. *Journal of Arts Management, Law, and Society*, 30(4), 268–282.

Bex, S., & Craps, S. (2016). Humanitarianism, testimony, and the white savior industrial complex: *What Is the What* versus *Kony 2012*. Cultural Critique, 92, 32.

Bing, R. (1972). *The memoirs of Sir Rudolf Bing: 5000 nights at the opera*. Doubleday and Company.

Bivens, D. K. (2005). What is internalized racism? In M. Potapchuk, S. Leiderman, D. Bivens, & B. Major (Eds.), *Flipping the script: White privilege and community building*, p. 44. www.racialequitytools.org/resourcefiles/What_is_Internalized_Racism.pdf.

Caplan, L. (2017). A small step toward correcting the overwhelming Whiteness of opera. *The New Yorker*. Accessed December 13, 2019. www.newyorker.com/culture/culture-desk/a-small-step-toward-correcting-the-overwhelming-whiteness-of-opera.

Cheatham, W. (1998). Black-male singers at the metropolitan opera. *Black Perspectives in Music*, 16(1), 3–20.

Cheatham, W. (1997). *Dialogues on opera and the African American experience*. Scarecrow Press.

Cooper, M. (2019). The Met will stage its first opera by a Black composer. *The New York Times*. Accessed December 13, 2019. www.nytimes.com/2019/09/19/arts/music/metropolitan-opera-black-composers-terence-blanchard.html?action=click&module=RelatedLinks&pgtype=Article.

Crawford, R. (2001). *America's musical life: A history*. Norton and Company.

Crenshaw, K., Gotanda, N., Peller, G., & Thomas, K. (1996). *Critical race theory: The key writings that formed the movement*. The New Press.

Cuyler, A. C. (2019). The role of foundations in achieving Creative Justice. *Grantmakers in the Arts Reader*, 30(1), 57–62.

Cuyler, A. C. (2007). *The careers of non-European executive opera administrators in the U.S.* [Unpublished doctoral dissertation]. Florida State University.

DiAngelo, R. J. (2018). *White fragility: Why it's so hard for White people to talk about racism.* Beacon Press.

Dizikes, J. (1993). *Opera in America: A cultural history.* Yale University Press.

Fey, W. H. (2018). *The US will become 'minority white' in 2045, Census projects.* www.brookings.edu/blog/the-avenue/2018/03/14/the-us-will-become-minority-white-in-2045-census-projects/.

Fiedler, J. (2001). *Molto agitato: The mayhem behind the music at the metropolitan opera.* Nan A. Talese.

Garre-Schmidt, J. (Director). (2000). *Aïda's brothers and sisters: Black voices in opera* [Documentary]. Kultur.

Heilbrun, J., & Gray, C.M. (2001). *The economics of art and culture.* Cambridge University Press.

Helicon Collaborative. (2017). *Not just money: Equity issues in cultural philanthropy.* https://heliconcollab.net/our_work/not-just-money/.

Henze, R. (2018). *Introduction to international arts management.* Springer VS.

Henze, R., & Wolfram, G. (2014). *Exporting culture: Which role for Europe in a global world?* Springer VS.

Hu, K. (2019). Classical opera has a racism problem. *The New York Times.* Accessed December 13, 2019. www.nytimes.com/2019/12/19/opinion/opera-racism-puccini.html?auth=login-google.

LeRoy, M. H. (2018). Targeting white supremacy in the workplace. *Stanford Law & Policy Review*, 29(1), 107–158.

Mayer, M. (1987). Sound ambitions, unsteady resources: Opera companies in the 1980s. *Journal of Arts Management, Law, and Society*, 17(1), 5–22.

McIntosh, P. (1989). White privilege: Unpacking the invisible knapsack. *Peace of Freedom Magazine.* Accessed December 13, 2019. https://nationalseedproject.org/Key-SEED-Texts/white-privilege-unpacking-the-invisible-knapsack.

Midgette, A. (2019). Russell Thomas is much more than a black tenor. Now, he's tackling 'Otello' and the field's stereotypes. *The Washington Post.* Accessed December 13, 2019. www.washingtonpost.com/entertainment/music/russell-thomas-is-much-more-than-a-black-tenor-now-hes-tackling-otello-and-the-fields-stereotypes/2019/10/16/0fc2b45c-eeac-11e9-8693-f487e46784aa_story.html?mc_cid=a639c83a51&mc_eid=4254e9122a.

National Endowment for the Arts. (2019). *U.S. patterns of arts participation: A full report from the 2017 survey of public participation in the arts.* Accessed December 13, 2019. www.arts.gov/sites/default/files/US_Patterns_of_Arts_ParticipationRevised.pdf.

National Endowment for the Arts. (2002). *2002 survey of public participation in the arts: Summary report.* NEA Research Division Report No. 45. National Endowment for the Arts.

OPERA America. (2020c). *About.* Accessed May 28, 2020. www.operaamerica. org/content/about/index.aspx.

OPERA America. (2020b). *Annual field report 2019.* Accessed May 28, 2020. www.operaamerica.org/files/oadocs/financials/FY18_AFR.pdf.

OPERA America. (2020a). *Report from the field with Marc A. Scorca.* Accessed May 28, 2020. www.youtube.com/watch?v=9IVW3HnmMk4&feature=youtu.be.

Public Broadcasting System (PBS). (2017). *White supremacy and terrorism.* Accessed December 13, 2019. www.pbs.org/tpt/slavery-by-another-name/themes/white-supremacy/.

Rivera, J. (2017). Opera in America: Is it circling the toilet? *The Huffington Post.* Accessed December 13, 2019. www.huffpost.com/entry/opera-in-america-is-it-ci_b_5005929.

Rushton, M. (2018). Why do we subsidize donations to the opera? *Cultural Trends, 27*(3), 160–172.

Sicca, L. (1997). The management of opera houses: The Italian experience of the Enti Autonomi. *International Journal of Cultural Policy, 4*(1), 201–224.

Sidford, H. (2011). *Fusing arts, culture and social change: High impact strategies for philanthropy.* Accessed December 13, 2019. http://heliconcollab.net/wp-content/uploads/2013/04/Fusing-Arts_Culture_and_Social_Change1.pdf.

Siefert, M. (2004). The Metropolitan Opera in the American century: Opera singers, Europe, and cultural politics. *Journal of Arts Management, Law, and Society, 33*(4), 298–315.

Smith, E. L. (1995). *Blacks in opera: An encyclopedia of people and companies, 1873–1993.* McFarland Press.

Steele, S. (2007). *White guilt: How Blacks and Whites together destroyed the promise of the civil rights era.* Harper Perennial.

Stein, T. S. (2020). *Racial and ethnic diversity in the performing arts workforce.* Routledge.

Stein, T. S. (2000). Creating opportunities for people of color in performing arts management. *Journal of Arts Management, Law, and Society, 29*(4), 304–318.

Story, R. M. (1990). *And so I sing: African American divas of opera and concert.* Warner Books Inc.

Straubhaar, R. (2015). The stark reality of the "White Saviour" complex and the need for critical consciousness: A document analysis of the early journals of a Freirean educator. *Compare: A Journal of Comparative and International Education, 45*(3), 381–400.

Super, D. E. (1957). *The psychology of careers: An introduction to vocational development.* Harper.

Super, D. E. (1953). A theory of vocation development. *American Psychologist, 8,* 185–190.

Volpe, J. (2006). *The toughest show on earth: My rise and reign at the Metropolitan Opera.* Knopf Publishing.

Waleson, H. (2018). *Mad scenes and exit arias: The death of the New York City Opera and the future of opera in America.* Metropolitan Books.

Walls, S. C. (2019). Opera by Black composers have long been ignored. Explore 8. *The New York Times*. Accessed December 13, 2019. www.nytimes.com/2019/09/19/arts/music/black-operas-composers.html?mc_cid=e29b9c31a6&mc_eid=4254e9122a.

Yusuf, J. (2016). The struggle of the veiled woman: 'White Savior Complex' and rising Islamophobia create a two-fold plight. *Harvard International Review*, 37(2), 51–54.

2 Act I: Henry Akina
From Stage Director to Artistic Director of Hawaii Opera Theatre

Born in 1965, Henry Akina is the only executive opera manager of color in the U.S. whose year of birth casts him as Generation X, or the group of people born between 1965 and 1979 (KASASA, 2019). He grew up in Hawaii, and early exposure to arts education played a major role in his career path. As a child he was very much into theater. In fact, as a boy he dreamed of becoming an actor. Mr. Akina stated, "the excitement of the theater was something that really inspired me at that time." But, a family member, his great uncle and grandmother's brother-in-law, served as chorus master at the MET (Metropolitan Opera), which also impacted his love for the theater. He grew up hearing his grandmother's stories of visiting backstage. Though his parents were medical professionals, Mr. Akina also listened to opera broadcasts with them. At six years old he saw his first opera, *Carmen*, at the Hawaii Opera Theatre (HOT). But, it was through seeing HOT's production of *Turandot* as a teenager that he realized that music could also provide a gateway to theater.

After receiving his Bachelor of Arts degree magna cum laude in Psychology and Drama from Tufts University in 1977, Mr. Akina moved to Germany to attend the Free University of Berlin, where he continued to study theater science by working as an assistant director. As we continued our interview, Mr. Akina revealed that pursuing a career in opera did not occur to him until he moved to Europe. Three opera companies were in existence during his time studying in Berlin. He stated, "it was a wonderful landscape to learn in."

After his studies, he co-founded the Berlin Chamber Opera company with a conductor in 1981 where he served as the primary director. With the company, he directed 50 opera productions including four world premieres. During this time, he also began teaching acting and performance skills to opera singers at the Conservatory of the Arts in West Berlin, a skill that would serve him well as General and Artistic Director at HOT. He believes that all of his experiences played a big role in helping him to get jobs, including his role at HOT.

In 1996, HOT's invitation to lead the staff served as a homecoming of sorts because he would now take on the primary leadership role in the company that had provided him with so many of his early experiences with opera. During our interview, Mr. Akina made it clear that he only worked in Hawaii and Berlin. He stated, "I don't know anything else." In his new role with HOT, he planned to produce more operatic activities throughout the year, expand the education program, and balance the repertoire between classics and new works. He felt that HOT could become a "cultural lighthouse in the community." He said in an interview highlighted in HOT's the *Tales of Henry*, "I wanted opera more for the people."

During his 30-year career as the first Hawaiian director of HOT, Mr. Akina directed more than 120 operas, and served as the Artistic Director of the company for 20 years. In 2015, the Hawaii Arts Alliance recognized Mr. Akina with its Alfred Preis Honor for his commitment to arts and arts education in Hawaii. The state legislature also awarded him a certificate for his lifelong service to the arts in 2016. But the legacy Mr. Akina is most proud of is the Mae Z. Orvis Opera studio, which provides opportunities and connections for young local singers to interact with professionals in the opera world. The studio is fully funded, and participants can enjoy its benefits free of charge. Studio members have ranged from college age to slightly older. Brilliantly, the studio has served as a mechanism to cultivate local talent that HOT has employed in its productions. In April 2017, Mr. Akina retired from the company, directing his final production, Offenbach's *The Tales of Hoffman*, with HOT.

When I asked him what strategies he would recommend an aspiring opera manager to use to chart a path to executive management, he shared the following response:

> I think that if you can study, you should with a program because they have productions and you're interested in productions. They have a lot of programs with a lot of European guests. I would expect that you would learn the basics of playing instruments and reading music. I suppose that anyone who came to me would know that to begin with. I certainly spent a lot of time playing music for myself so that I could pick up a score and read it, you can see around the room there are lots of scores. I think that's an important part of it, but I don't think that's all of it.

I also asked Mr. Akina what, more if anything, can OPERA America do to assist the development of more executive opera managers of color. He replied:

> I don't know that they can do anything because you have to be at a certain level to get into OPERA America to begin with. I think that anyone who is interested should try and then ascend through the ranks that way. But, I don't know that OPERA America can do anything from where it sits now because they are making grants. Well, they could do things with the grant programs, but, I don't think that they could do a lot. From where they're positioned now in the operatic landscape.

As we closed our interview, I took in the view of Mr. Akina's living room, and indeed he had several bookshelves full of scores and lots of opera memorabilia. Seeing his library inspired me to ask him, what is his favorite opera? He replied, "my favorite opera is Wagner's *Tristan und Isolde.*" Of course I asked, why? He replied that the central conflict is one that is dear to his heart, particularly the love between Tristan and Isolde, and the relationship with King Mark makes a perfect triangle. He continued, "it is the perfection of the score that really speaks to me." Curious to know if he had ever directed a production of the opera, I asked, "In your career did you ever get to direct a production of *Tristan und Isolde?*" He replied, "Only once in Hawaii, and it was an experience because it was the first time they produced Wagner there." I found this incredibly interesting given that music historians continue to debate Wagner's anti-Semitic views and the musical inspiration he provided to the third Reich. Perhaps this, too, supports the rationale for the need for more executive opera managers of color who may help to bridge the racial divides across communities using opera. According to Americans for the Arts (2018), 72% of U.S. citizens believe that the arts unify communities regardless of age, race, and ethnicity.

Although I am utterly fascinated by all of the respondents in this book, I consider it a personal triumph that Mr. Akina agreed to allow me to interview him. First, because, as he has publicly stated, his doctor had diagnosed him with a progressive neurological disorder. This explains why this particular chapter is shorter than the others. Although I asked him the same questions as all of the respondents, I did not want to tax Mr. Akina for longer responses. Second, because when I first asked him to participate in the initial study that serves as the basis for this book over ten years ago, he said, "no." He took issue with the study because of its title, "The Career Paths of Non-European American Executive Opera Administrators in the U.S." Mr. Akina argued that as someone of Chinese, Hawaiian, and German descent, he did not fit the parameters set forth for the study. He also forthrightly asked, "why do discussions of race always emanate from the Eastern seaboard of the U.S.?" Nevertheless, this time around he said, "yes," and that he appreciated and understood my intentions.

References

Americans for the Arts. (2018). *Americans speak out about the arts in 2018: An in-depth look at perceptions and attitudes about the arts in America.* Accessed December 13, 2019. www.americansforthearts.org/sites/default/files/Public%20Opinion%20National%202018%20Report.pdf.

Hawaii Opera Theatre. *The Tales of Henry.* Accessed December 13, 2019. www.hawaiiopera.org/news-events/tales-henry/#sthash.kvOhzHMQ.kXHweh8q.dpbs.

KASASA. (2019). *Boomers, Gen X, Gen Y, and Gen Z explained.* www.kasasa.com/articles/generations/gen-x-gen-y-gen-z.

3 Act II: Torrie Allen

From Singer to General/Artistic Director of Anchorage Opera

Torrie Allen was born on June 5, 1964 in El Paso, Texas on Fort Bliss military base. His father was from a little steel town outside of Pittsburgh, Pennsylvania, and his mother was from Louisville, Kentucky. Due to his father serving in World War II and the Korean War, he grew up in a military family. Because his father did not want to continue his military service in Vietnam, he decided to retire. This prompted the family's move to the San Francisco bay area. Mr. Allen's family lived in Berkeley, California for a year, and then moved to Concord, California where he grew up in a town outside of San Francisco.

He attended public schools in California, at a time when the public schools experimented with a magnet program for gifted students. He entered that program, which he credits for increasing his exposure to the arts and science, in the third grade. His experience in that program encouraged his fascination with what happens off stage relative to the preparation and the stewarding of the performing arts. This fascination has remained with him throughout his career, and likely unconsciously influenced his decision to transition from singer to opera manager.

Mr. Allen also grew up in a family of performers. In the early 1970s, the younger generation of Mr. Allen's mother's family enjoyed brief and modest success in the pop world. He credits his family as among the first to blend rock and gospel music in the U.S. The family's group used the stage name *The Stovall Sisters* (Edwards, 2019). The group's seminal album, *The Stovall Sisters*, featured one of the family's oldest songs, "Spirit in the Sky." The group worked with a White producer who took their song and went on to make millions from it. This story impacted Mr. Allen deeply; he stated:

> That experience made me aware of what happens to people if they don't understand the business of the arts. My aunts (*The Stovall Sisters*) ended up not doing very well and struggling and this fellow

took a family song. I hear the song often. Portions of the work are consistently used as soundtrack material for a variety of commercial products, cars, and movies.

Mr. Allen noted that this reminded him to remain aware of this system that takes advantage of people who are not aware of their leverage:

> It's great to be on stage. It's great to sing. But how do you run this business, also? There's a fascinating history of African Americans early on in this country having to do both and learning to have both skills. They were recitalists and they learned to manage themselves as businesses.

As the time came for Mr. Allen to attend college, he went to UCLA having already established an identity as a rock musician. He recounted the story of meeting one of his first counselors at UCLA. The counselor told him that if he wanted to attend Law school, which he hoped to do after his undergraduate studies, he would need to have as many diverse experiences as possible to become an attractive prospect. As a result, he joined the Men's Glee Club at UCLA. He credited Donn Weiss (Music Director of the Men's Glee Club) for inquiring about his interest in singing solos, which led to other faculty realizing that he had a remarkable singing voice. He recounted this story to describe the inspiration for his singing voice:

> As a kid, I have a very strong memory with my mom, watching a TV show called *Gomer Pyle* and hearing the actor playing Gomer, Jim Nabors, sing "The Impossible Dream." And, there was another show. It was the *Dinah Shore Show*. On one episode, Robert Goulet sang "If Ever I Would Leave You." As a kid, I remember locking into the deep, dark, and bright timbre of those two voices and wanting to have that kind of a sound. So, 20 years later I'm at UCLA and I'm thinking, "Hmm. Maybe I can tap into that seed that was planted 20 years ago when I heard these guys sing?" So, that's how it started.

From there, Weiss and others suggested that he consider singing opera. Mr. Allen's family also had a successful friend who grew up among opera singers. This friend's parents, however, forced him to study medicine. This friend eventually became very financially successful. Mr. Allen bene-fitted from his generosity because the family friend agreed to become a major patron if he wanted to pursue a career in opera. Mr. Allen's voice teacher at UCLA, John Guarnieri, encouraged him to accept the offer and go to the East Coast to audition for various conservatories. Boston Conservatory accepted him and he decided to enroll because of the small cohort of students.

At this time, he had no background in opera or classical music. But, because he had supporters, he decided to explore the possibilities. It took him a year to learn to appreciate the art form and to begin to learn about opera's history. In his exploration of the art form, he began to learn about African Americans in opera such as Paul Robeson, Robert McFerrin, Jules Bledsoe, Sissieretta Jones, Roland Hayes, and Leontyne Price. He wanted to learn as much as he could about all of the African American singers. He particularly wanted to know about what happened to them. Then, he discovered and studied the operatic basses such as George London, Martti Talvela, Kim Borg, Cesare Siepi, Simon Estes, and Samuel Ramey, whose teacher (Armen Boyajian) he studied with for ten years.

By 1998, Mr. Allen's career in opera had begun to flourish. Foretelling his interest in management, Mr. Allen relayed a story about how during a visit at the Royal Opera House in Madrid, Spain, he had a profound awareness that he had more interest in talking with the marketing and development people than spending time with the performers. He wondered about managing a big opera house in a big European city. He relayed that he has always had a fascination with the impresario's perspective. Although his singing career progressed well, it became confusing and uncomfortable for him. He recounted:

> My patrons were saying things to me like, "We're offering you the silver spoon." But I grew up in a modest home and didn't know how to take full advantage of their patronage.

Nevertheless, he was now enmeshed in the opera world. In addition to learning all the languages, he also had to learn the mores that go along with an opera career. In 1998, he debuted at the Brengenz Festpiel in Austria (*Porgy and Bess*). After that, he came back to the U.S. and auditioned for the Metropolitan Opera Guild, which he won. But after the audition, he received a call from his agent that the Guild's orchestra planned to go on strike. This led to a critical epiphany; he stated:

> I had been doing it for about ten years... and I thought, "I don't know if I'm cut out for the nomadic lifestyle of a professional singer." The day that I auditioned for the Met Guild, I was downstairs at the Metropolitan Opera. I was singing one of Figaro's arias

from the *Marriage of Figaro*. While I was singing, I had a weird out-of-body experience. I was thinking to myself, "I'm not in character right now. I'm just singing a song. I don't know if I want to do this." Plácido Domingo and Denise Graves were directly above me rehearsing *Samson and Delilah*, and I was saying to myself, "I just wanted to know that I had the chops to get to this level. I don't want this life anymore. I want more from the arts."

After this epiphany, Mr. Allen made some major career changes in his life. He lamented that he felt like he did not have enough control because in opera, one is always at the mercy of some director's vision. He also felt that opera lacked a plethora of different voices in its conceptualization, particularly as a Euro-centric art form. He did not want to get trapped in what began to feel like a bubble. In addition, he needed more ways to express himself. During our interview, he made it clear that he loves opera, but the art form has not maximized its viability or vibrancy; he stated, "It doesn't have to be dying."

After making the career decision to move into arts leadership, Mr. Allen started thinking about what he really liked. But, he also thought about the behaviors and practices that he did not like:

> When you're on the road and you're singing, and you see those instances of your colleagues being taken advantage of because someone in power has some curious sexual fantasy. That was so common. As far as I'm concerned, the #MeToo movement is long overdue.

About this time, he discovered Opera Ebony of New York City. He worked closely with the leaders (Ben Matthews and Wayne Sanders) for two years. He described having a nonprofit management job during the day, and then spending the evenings at Opera Ebony volunteering administrative support, receiving coaching, performing, and learning about the industry.

I recounted remembering a project that Opera Ebony spearheaded that led to the documentary, *Aïda's Brothers and Sisters*. With a great deal of excitement, he exclaimed:

> Yes! We helped put that together with some European producers. What I brought to them (Opera Ebony) was energy. I felt that because I had been singing for ten years, I had to make up time. I needed to learn as much as I could without delay. I was hungry. What they gave me was wisdom and knowledge. For instance, when

I was an opera singer and participated in educational outreach programs, sometimes we'd go to communities of color and the young
African American kids would ask me, "Why are you singing opera?"
I would just say, "Well, I like to sing it." From the folks at Opera
Ebony, I learned that what we call opera today is a variation of an
expressive form that has existed for thousands of years. Western
music history books claim that opera was born in Europe in the
1500s. This is untrue. I grew to understand that I was singing opera
because it was deeply encoded in my DNA.

Mr. Allen talked about how many African American singers saw Opera
Ebony as ground zero for their careers. Through his volunteer work with
Opera Ebony, he learned about the stories and the systemic racism
African American opera singers faced:

Beyond overt instances of racism, from my perspective, the real problem was the overwhelming amount of constant micro-aggressions.
And the sad thing about the micro-aggressions is that a lot of good
folk really didn't see themselves and their actions as aggressive. It was
a horrible state of affairs that hurt performers of color and diminished
the potential vibrancy of the entire industry. It was painful to hear
stories about how the accumulation of this stuff made some people
literally go crazy. I would hear things like folks having nervous break-
downs because of having to wear White makeup or having to negotiate
shocking levels of sexual harassment. I had to wear White makeup.
They'd say, oh, if you want to sing this role in this production, you're
going to have to wear White makeup. Ugly, brutal… and it was really
happening… as recently as the 1990s!

Mr. Allen also shared these two stories to further illustrate his point
about systemic racism in opera:

I'll never forget this one time at the Chautauqua Institute's opera
program when a well-meaning coach said to me, "You shouldn't do
Figaro, 'cause the king of Spain, would never have an African as his
barber." And the more I researched and studied, "Absolutely, he
would!" I remember doing a studio artist opera program in Sar-
asota, Florida when the Artistic Director said to me, "You're here
because of the EEOC requirements."

Furthermore, he discussed some of the challenges he faced at Opera
Ebony due to a combination of Founder's Syndrome (BoardSource,

2016), residual trauma from experiencing racism, and his own immaturity. Oftentimes, he felt that his mentors did not share his vision for Opera Ebony; he stated:

> I would say to them, "Let's go big and commercial. I want the world to know about you and for you to serve as a wedge for newness in the industry." My youthful enthusiasm was met with resistance. Now, I get it. They had a purpose that was more sublime and important than my personal visions.

Still, he values his time with Opera Ebony because through volunteering with them he gained valuable insights serving as their General Manager pro bono for a couple of years doing development, PR, marketing, and administration.

As he retold the story of attending his first OPERA America conference after becoming Executive and Artistic Director of Anchorage Opera, I could hear the excitement about possibilities in his voice:

> I was all excited about it. I'd just become the Executive and Artistic Director of the Anchorage Opera and the first African American to lead a major performing arts organization in the U.S. circumpolar north. Soon after accepting the position, I attended my first OPERA America conference. During the first luncheon and there were more than 1,200 folks in attendance. I walked in and was immediately struck by the fact that I may have been the only African American in the place. My next thought was, "This is why they keep programming *Porgy and Bess*." This industry is frighteningly homogeneous off the stage. At the same time, I didn't feel unwelcome. In that moment, I could see "This is the problem. This is it. The lack of diversity behind the scenes." I had a similar experience in 2000 at my first Association for Performing Arts Presenters (APAP) conference.

Though this could have discouraged some other people of color, it convinced Mr. Allen that he had to continue this path. He expressed that more people of color have to begin to work behind the scenes and talk about all the other beautiful work out there and the beautiful composers out there and the other stories. If opera continues as it has, he lamented, "We'll be doing *Porgy and Bess* another 100 years from now."

He is convinced that opera suffers from a lack of different voices, particularly when it comes to artistic and administrative staff. He expressed that it was so clear at his first OPERA America conference. He shared an additional story related to this point, when he said:

There was a fellow from North Carolina. He came up to me and said, "Do you feel like the white elephant here?" I said, "Wow. That's interesting." We had both just attended a session on diversity. He goes, "And you're the only Black person." I said, "No, I don't feel out of place." Marc Scorca, who was and still is the President of OPERA America, exemplified the welcoming spirit. His proactive goodness neutralized any potential otherness anxiety about the situation. Scorca was always very supportive. I felt nothing but support from him. However, there is an issue, a systemic issue, a profound unconscious (and conscious) bias, that needs deeper analysis and active shifting.

He believes that the opera world has missed out on too many wonderful opportunities to energize and make the art form relevant. He believes that OPERA America's President, Mark Scorca, has his heart in the right place and is very forward-thinking, but there's so much self-defeating legacy energy in the industry.

Opera's inability to boldly step into the future also hinders it from creating a variety of entry points for those outside of the exclusive opera fan club. He shared a disturbing story about how his colleagues responded to him disclosing that he had plans to program the Zarzuela, *La Tabernera del Puerto*, in a breakout session for General Managers during his second OPERA America conference. He shared this:

> I said to my colleagues, "I'm gonna do a Zarzuela. I found this really cool Zarzuela, *La Tabernera del Puerto* (the tavern girl on the port). It's really cool. The music is fabulous. It's relevant. The folks in Alaska are going to like it." I think there were ten of us in the group. Some of them started laughing. A few started gossiping with each other, like, "Oh, this guy's crazy. He's gonna do a Zarzuela?" I thought to myself, "Wow, they are so comfortable with bias." Now, they weren't racist, but clearly what they were doing is manifesting a systemic racism. I was disappointed and wanted to say (but didn't), "You guys are killing the industry." What's wrong with the opera world trying to make itself relevant, I mean, the automotive industry is constantly remaking itself. We're not driving 1920 Fords, right? In the opera world, we're still driving 1920 Fords. Occasionally some new car will surface and you think that's gonna change things, but it doesn't...

Yet, he believes that opera can make this much-needed evolution. However, the gravity of legacy may make achieving this evolution exceedingly difficult. He shared this anecdote regarding managing the gravity of legacy:

> So, when you're actually running the company, you've gotta deal with boards and you've got to deal with the community. And when you start changing stuff, you have to have mentors who are there to say to you, "Look. It's okay to change. You're gonna get some pushback. That's okay. Don't get scared. Keep going." And if there is not enough of those kind of mentors, that can prepare people, change mentors, that can make people feel comfortable. Fear and stasis will prevail. I've learned that it is possible to negotiate this change. If one embraces the diplomatic mindset and related techniques, it may take a little bit longer and require more patience, but you can take people and communities from A to B.

When the conversation turned to the issue of racism and systemic biases, of the six respondents in this book, Mr. Allen is one of two who shared an instance where he thought he had encountered professional racism. He provided the examples below to affirm the systemic and implicit bias that can oftentimes leave people of color wondering, "What just happened?"

> I'll give you a couple of examples. One example is with a well-known opera agent. I was leading Anchorage Opera. We were in New York City auditioning singers, our Musical Director's there, I'm there. I sensed that a lot of the agents and singers were surprised to see me (a person of color) behind the table. I mean, I don't think that they knew that I had just as much or more real-life training and professional performance experience than them. This well-known agent came in and he's looking at my Musical Director. And right there in front of me, he's saying to him, "Watch out for these people." I was like, "What?" It was so shocking that I didn't act then. As I reflect on it now, I should've just asked him to leave then. It was so unbelievably disrespectful, racist, and all that is bad about the legacy mindset.

Mr. Allen went on to express that this agent would probably never think of himself as a racist, behavior commonly understood as *Whitesplaining* (Dictionary.com, 2020). But, in Mr. Allen's view, this exchange represented the epitome of unconscious and implicit racial bias. He stated again, "It's a manifestation of systemic bias." To think that an agent felt comfortable enough to make such a comment does not surprise me. In many ways for people of color, particularly when they enter spaces that are majority White, this is simply par the course.

Instead of internalizing this racism as something of his own doing, Mr. Allen views it quite differently:

> I'm passionate about the arts. I also believe my way to change the world, to manifest Martin Luther King Jr.'s dream, is through the arts. That's how I do it. When it comes to our species and how we interact with each other, I want a world where we value curiosity above fear.

The second example below revealed the potential mindset of donors, who by and large in opera are White.

> I had a really interesting conversation with some donors. They work at Microsoft and they were high-end donors at the Oregon Shakespeare Festival. They said, "We used to give all of our extra money to political campaigns, but we realize what's happening down in Oregon is so powerful and so important that by giving our money to you, it's gonna have a bigger impact for this country."

He believes that opera suffers from not attracting enough individuals like this, folks with a deep analysis. He stated, "There aren't that many of them out there." While he categorized Marc Scorca as one of them, he expressed that Marc is one person. He stated, "Thank god, he's the leader of OPERA America, but I think if more 'woke' folk supported him, it would help." In yet another, more hope-inspiring example, he shared the following:

> I had a funder tell me, "You know, I was really against all this Equity, Inclusion, and Diversity stuff," and she said to me, "I was racist. I had some racist views. I come from a racist family. However, after attending some racial awareness and equity sessions, I realized that race is just a social construct. I get it now. I've had such a big mental breakthrough. Like, how we label people." Just think of all the beautiful relationships I've deprived myself of, my family has deprived themselves of because we were victims of this social construct. "Just think of all the beautiful opportunities we deprived ourselves of." I think, well, that's what's happening in opera and the performing arts. So many beautiful opportunities are missed when you don't reflect all of humanity.

Towards the end of our interview, the topic turned to mentorship. Similar to every respondent in this book, Mr. Allen clearly benefitted from mentorship. Certainly, Ben Matthews (Director, Opera Ebony) and Lyndon Woodside (Music Director, Oratorio Society of New York) served as valuable mentors, but also the counselor who encouraged him to diversify his activities to make himself a more desirable candidate for Law school. When I asked if he was currently mentoring anyone he shared this:

> Yes, my staff and other young folk I intersect with. I've had good leaders and not-so-good leaders. I try my best to improve on the modeling from the very best leaders, because the not-so-good leaders really can have a toxic impact on your psyche. I just try to be as positive and encouraging as possible. I often ask my staff if they feel like I'm empowering them enough. Above and beyond this, I champion efforts to open doors for new voices and ideas. At Anchorage Opera, I recall wondering "How do I get more singers of color here?" They weren't showing up at the auditions. Then it dawned on me, "There aren't any agents of color, so there's probably some bias in how the agents are picking their singers."

In response to Mr. Allen sharing that singers of color did not show up to audition for Anchorage Opera, I asked him if he thought he would have had a different response if he had managed the Atlanta Opera? He stated, "I probably would've had access to more people of color. But, more is needed. More variation behind the scenes. I'm not sure if there would have been a measurable difference in that regard."

When our conversation turned towards the current attention that the U.S. cultural sector gives to ADEI, Mr. Allen and I discussed practices that trouble us. One of which is the mass adoption of ADEI statements without regard for the tremendous amount of work that needs to happen to ensure seismic change. Below, he shared the results of some of the volunteer work that he has done with a national organization:

> I serve on a committee with the National Arts Strategies and we've been working on a kind of an umbrella for this work. One of the things that we came up with together was: The social construct of race is deeply ingrained in our national and personal psyches. The long journey of equity analysis and reflection will reveal how we're all victimized by the divisive mythology of race, and how we can begin the individual and group work needed to free our minds of its limitations. The journey will include hard, yet breakthrough and life-changing conversations that may trigger misunderstanding, confusion, and unconscious emotions. Therefore, we must always start with and remain firmly grounded in a commitment to safe,

non-conflict-avoiding, non-judgmental, and grace-filled space for every person and every perspective. What we hope to encourage is organizations to move beyond the meaningless diversity statements. Also, we hope to inspire institutional funders to make more meaningful work in the area a priority. I feel like there needs to be greater levels of accountability around this stuff.

Because of OPERA America's leadership role in the field, I asked what more could they do to encourage the change the cultural sector seeks to make regarding racial ADEI. Mr. Allen responded:

> Move beyond diversity statements, as soon as possible! Grow to understand the links between ADEI, relevance, and greater economic impact. Apply ADEI filters to all aspects of the business, not just for what's happening on stage or for show. I often witness situations where there's much hoopla about public-facing equity gestures from folk who score very low in this regard on their own turf, in their work spaces and management practices. We should demand sincerity and call out the imposters, especially the falsely celebrated imposters. We must do this work in a way that is sincere yet non-judgmental. Folks will avoid these conversations if they feel like they're gonna be judged or criticized. This is not about judging. This is about getting to a better place. Systemic bias is so sublimely ingrained as "normal" in our individual and collective psyches. If we don't preface the work this way, folks will be less likely to enter into conversation.

In closing, I asked Mr. Allen the question, "What is opera missing out on by having so few executive managers of color?" He responded with the following: new stories, new ways of telling the classic stories, and the vitality and vibrancy that comes with greater variations of sensitivity and experience. He currently serves as the President & CEO of Arts Midwest.

References

BoardSource. (2016). *Founder's syndrome.* Accessed December 13, 2019. https:// boardsource.org/resources/founders-syndrome/.

Dictionary.com. (2020). *Whitesplain.* Accessed May 28, 2020. www.dictionary. com/e/slang/whitesplain/.

Edwards, G. (2019). *20 R&B albums Rolling Stone loved in the 1970s you never heard.* Accessed December 13, 2019. www.rollingstone.com/music/music-lists/ 20-rb-albums-rolling-stone-loved-in-the-1970s-you-never-heard-164007/the-stovall-sisters-the-stovall-sisters-166731/.

4 Act III: Wayne Brown

From Orchestra Manager to President & CEO of Michigan Opera Theatre

Wayne Brown was born in Buffalo, New York, and spent his first seven or eight years there until his family moved to Detroit. He recalled the importance early exposure to arts education had on his career development by citing arts educators of import. He stated:

> Miss Martin was my music teacher in the fourth grade. This was in the public schools of Detroit, Winterhalter School. I remember my first violin classes in elementary school. Then another early influence in elementary school was my art teacher where we had the opportunity of working with sculpture. That too played an early influence. The third component was an involvement with the stage crew.

Clearly, early exposure to arts education through the Detroit public schools fostered the idea of participating in the arts. Unknowingly, the steps that followed had less to do with pursuing a career in opera and more to do with the fact that he enjoyed singing and group activities. In addition to arts education, Mr. Brown was active in his local church, junior achievement, Boy Scouts, and as a newspaper carrier. He relayed this story about his experience:

> I was a newspaper carrier. Owning my own, mini business was all part of my journey. I had my first trip to Florida, my first airplane flight, my first time going to Washington. All of that was the result of being a Detroit newspaper carrier and having been selected as one of the 30 top newspaper carriers in the city, and the end result was a three-day, all-expense paid trip to be the guest of the Detroit Tigers.

During our interview, he made a connection to that time and the location of the offices of the Michigan Opera Theatre. In fact, we could see Comerica Field, the home of the Detroit Tigers, from his office window.

Coming home to Detroit to serve as the President and CEO of Michigan Opera Theatre is full circle for Mr. Brown. All of the experiences communicated to him the whole notion of networking, creating new relationships, and leveraging early arts experiences in ways that he had no idea how they would manifest. Unlike many people who are gifted, he did not know what he wanted to do in the arts as it related to having a career.

Later on, in middle school, when he played the violin, he switched to cello because he thought that it would allow him to get to know a young lady better. As a result of transitioning to cello, he received the opportunity to study privately with Kemper Harreld who had just left Morehouse College where he led the Morehouse Glee Club. In high school, however, he directed his interest to vocal music. Though playing cello led him to joining the Detroit High School Honors Orchestra and Choir. He also attended performances of the Metropolitan Opera when they came to Detroit. He shared this story about meeting the first Black tenor to sing a leading role at the Met (Metropolitan Opera), George Shirley:

> During one visit, my high school choral director invited George Shirley, who was featured in one of the performances during the Met's visit; she extended an invitation for him to perform, to come out to our school, Mackenzie High School. The performance of the Russian Picnic was the ensemble work. George wanted to know who was the tenor who was featured in the work and I raised my hand. He said, "I would like to hear Wayne Brown sing the solo role that I'm expected to sing," to see if I might learn something.

Hearing an opera performance and seeing George Shirley in a direct role conveyed the message to him that opera is an extraordinary experience. After high school, Mr. Brown attended the University of Michigan where he served in a number of roles with the Men's Glee Club including conductor, business manager, Vice President, and President.

During his time as a voice major and business minor, he had the opportunity to manage the summer opera when the Assistant Dean accepted a position at another institution. The Dean asked Mr. Brown if he would take on this role because of his experience with the Men's Glee Club. Because of his management of Cimarosa's, the *Scarlet Letter*, income exceeded expenses, the audience met capacity, and he had a remarkable artistic experience. Due to his success, the Dean asked him if he had considered a career in Arts Management. He shared this response to the Dean's question, but also an example of the quality of mentorship he received from the Dean:

I said no, what is that? That was before the formalized programs at Columbia and North Texas and any number of places. Then the Detroit Symphony Orchestra opened; the Dean said to me, "If you are interested I'm glad to suggest that they speak with you." I went in for an interview; I was offered the opportunity to join the Detroit Symphony right out of completing my Bachelor's degree. However, I was about to take the Michigan Men's Glee Club on tour to the West Coast for three weeks. Then the executive director said, "When you return, let's continue."

After the tour, Mr. Brown served as administrative assistant, and then two years later assistant manager of the Detroit Symphony. He remained in the position for four years. Then he moved to Massachusetts where he managed his first orchestra. After six years there, he moved to Louisville, Kentucky. In Kentucky, he acquired the experience of managing a larger orchestra, focused on commissioning new works, and recording. Following that, he became the music producer at the Olympiad during the Olympic Games. He served as a panelist for the National Endowment for the Arts (NEA), which then led to his appointment as the Director of Music and Opera at the NEA. There, opera became a part of his portfolio. His responsibility for managing the portfolio on behalf of the United States government for music, including orchestra, chamber music, music festivals, and opera companies, brought him closer to the art form. During this time, the artistry of Leontyne Price, Kathleen Battle, among other incredible artists, informed and inspired his work. Nevertheless, a meeting with operatic icon David DiChiera would encourage his decision to transition into opera management. He told this story about that meeting:

> As it turns out, David DiChiera was the founder of Michigan Opera Theater. He and I had coffee a few years ago. He shared with me his plan to step down, and he wondered if I might have some suggestions of people he might work with. I gave him a list of four or five people. Six months later we re-visited along with his board chair, and I'm now with the Michigan Opera Theater and my role is President & CEO. It was not necessarily a pursuit to run an opera company early on. It culminated in this lifelong journey and interest in the opera field grew. It was a natural attraction and to be part of the company and to succeed someone like Dave DiChiera who had an unprecedented tenure, 47 years. In this country it's unprecedented. For me it's an honor to do what I do and to see how Michigan Opera Theater, and other opera companies, can play a

vital role within their communities to honor the master works, but to provide a platform so that today's stories will resonate with current audiences.

For some, Mr. Brown's professional appointments may similarly take the winding journey that becomes one's career. Though it appeared that Mr. Brown masterfully navigated a professional career in Arts Management, as a Black American man, I was curious to know what may have impeded his career, if anything at all. He responded by saying the following:

> Well, I would respond by saying that along the way I knew that I wanted to do something meaningful in the arts, but I was not always sure what that would be. I wouldn't necessarily say it impeded. Perhaps there were steps that I was introduced to various options along the way, which might have otherwise enabled me to have made a decision sooner than later. But, I think ultimately it all helped to better inform a better appreciation for what I do now. So I don't necessarily see any distractions along the way. I don't necessarily think of them as derailing, but indeed helping to enrich, enliven the curiosity and the interest, the passion for what I do.

To realize a highly successful executive career in Arts Management, Mr. Brown used a skillset that included having an understanding of the art form, networking, and passion. I wanted to know from his perspective what advice or strategies would he suggest a person pursuing a career in opera management use to manage their careers. Mr. Brown provided this advice:

> I would encourage anyone who's interested in, since we're talking about an arts arena, to learn as much as you can about the art form. That comes about through reading; it comes about through experiencing. Whether that's performance or other arts settings. Networking is critical. Being patient, and yet tenacious, and taking full advantage of every step along the way. To absorb and schedule informational interviews. Quite often people think in terms of interviews have to be job related, but interviews can be invaluable in terms of obtaining insight from those to whom you'd like to be better informed about the nature of their work. There are areas outside of the art world that can be equally informative. How to manage a business. Working on your interpersonal skills, making sure there's effective communication. Managing projects. Immersing

yourself in various cultures and languages. I would say those who have, perhaps a strong interest in the law, there are roles that can be played for someone who has a law degree. Increasingly, if we think about licensing and union contracts, those are all areas that can be of benefit to someone who's involved in Arts Management or in the role of leadership with an opera company.

Mentorship is a key strategy Mr. Brown and all of the respondents in this book used to attain their executive careers in opera. However, in general, the extent to which aspiring or emerging arts managers benefit from mentorship remains a serious question for cultural organizations. Perhaps, this is because for the first time in U.S. society, five generations live and work among each other (Grensing-Pophal, 2018), which may cause competition for opportunities. When I asked Mr. Brown if he were currently mentoring anyone, he shared:

My response would be not in an official way. I have regular conversations with any number of individuals who are at various stages in their pursuit of what we do, and even those who are actively managing organizations. I have not, per se, tried to identify a specific person to whom I wish to devote sole attention, but I think it's something that I'd be curious to do more. In fact I've been asked to participate in a couple of seminars and work with a few Master's students on this very topic.

As the service arts organization for opera, I wanted to gain an understanding on insights Mr. Brown had about OPERA America's role in addressing the lack of diversity among executives in opera companies. He shared this response:

I happen to be a member of the OPERA America board, and I consider for that reason my responsibility as a member of the board, and as a member of OPERA America, and as a head of an opera company to encourage and to be a part of and join forces with my colleagues to raise attention, to be committed to increasing opportunities for participation in our art form, not only in terms of upper management but throughout the entire organization. Whether that is at the governing body, at a staff level, volunteers, whether that's audience, I think we benefit from a holistic approach, as opposed to necessarily thinking about a particular slot or a particular role. To the degree that we can increase the participation broadly, then we start to nurture more of a network for those who want to take on

various roles. I think it's as important to focus on the board leadership as I do for the artistic or executive leadership of a company, or the artistic position of who's on the podium, who's on the
stage, among our significant donors. I think that's the role that
OPERA America can play. It's leadership's role to try to nurture,
to convey the importance that our companies become much more
reflective of the communities we serve, and that through fellowships, that may be paid fellowships, may be unpaid fellowships.
It's about creating an environment which values diversity, equity,
and inclusion. Creating an environment that focuses not only on
artistic works of what we refer to as the core repertoire, but the
inclusion of works that speak to current-day audiences and current-day concerns and interests. It's that holistic view which I think
OPERA America can continue to build on in this area. Each year
I'm seeing incremental growth and outreach to engage broadly in
communities that are not otherwise participating in a meaningful
way in our communities.

In this discussion, I pushed back a bit because as it currently stands, he is
the only person of color serving as an executive opera manager, when
ten years ago five people of color managed opera companies in the U.S.
at the executive level. However, Mr. Brown expressed that he thought
my focus on executives was too narrow; he remarked:

Whether it's one or 50, for me that is an incomplete focus. That's
why I would say, what is an institution's commitment to the art
form and its community? In 2005, Michigan Opera Theater hosted
an OPERA America conference in Detroit. I came out for that and
I raised the question, "You're going to have, as a result, the issues
of how one addresses diversity and inclusion in very different
ways." Diversity of perspective. Diversity of thought. Not necessarily just ethnic. Diversity in cultures. The work that has taken
place over the last five years, especially, I have seen enormous
growth of thought, perspective, program design, and investment by
OPERA America over these last few years, than I have in decades. I
think these issues evolve over time, and I would also say that
having been on the league's board for a number of years I've seen
how the fellowship programs have gone through cycles. Here in
Detroit we happen to have the headquarters for the Sphinx Organization and I've seen how that has evolved over time. I think it
has more to do with organizations, as they redefine themselves, as
cultural shifts occur, as we continue to struggle in terms of what

defines community. I think that OPERA America has committed itself to working with its members. We have to remember that the service organizations can provide the guidance. Ultimately, it comes down to the member organizations, how they choose to move forward.

Mr. Brown further went on to describe that the Detroit Symphony Orchestra is framed as the most accessible orchestra on the planet. This remains an institutional goal for the orchestra. Mr. Brown does not believe that Detroit's case is an ideal scenario for an organization in another city or state. He further contended that the role the service arts organizations play is to align a commitment to the art form, a commitment to community, a commitment to demonstrating how communities can use the art form as a platform. He stated the following:

> It can be an incredible platform for the community to convey its message. Prime example, the opera we're closing with this week is an initiative based in parks and sports which focuses on *The Summer King*, an opera about National Negro League player, Josh Gibson. It's designed to bring arts and sports together, which goes beyond the issue of, it happens to have a particular theme about Josh Gibson, but it's a step that we believe is attracting interest and participation which goes outside the arts community. It goes to the community more broadly. These are really complex issues and I think we benefit from a holistic approach to approaching these opportunities.

In response, I suggested to Mr. Brown that for some who have been in the fight for ADEI in the cultural sector there has been too little progress, which is defeating and disenfranchising. He replied:

> I think that's been community specific, I think that's been institution specific. There are those where perhaps there haven't been any changes. There are others where there's been a pretty robust shift. When I think about the body of new work for opera companies, when I think about ten years ago we could look at the number of new works, broadly, then we look at the number of new works by people of color, we can look at new works, where are they occurring, what are their platforms? It's really community specific. I think that that's just a reality. The work that takes place by our service arts organization should always be ahead of its field. That's the leadership role. When I think about the dance sector, the dance

experience, there's ballet being one aspect of dance, there are other dance platforms, and that will also tend to be, whether or not it's dance reflective of specific cultures, whether it's Ballet Hispanico, whether it's Alvin Ailey, whether it's just any number of platforms. Dance probably has been much more at the heart of a cultural experience within the community already than opera or chamber music. I don't know that they necessarily have to all be equal. I don't know that it's practical that they can all be equal. But nurturing greater participation, so it's not just who's in the front office, but nurturing more artistic administrators. Nurturing the careers for orchestra operations managers. Nurturing careers so we have greater participation among the trustees and our board. That for me matters. David DiChiera had an incredible track record getting careers going. Kathleen Battle received her first professional opera experience here in Detroit. Maria Ewing, Leona Mitchell they all came out of the experience in Detroit. It's not because David DiChiera was African American. It's because he had a commitment to diversity and inclusion. There are those who are going to be the agents of change. I don't know that, when you consider the scale of the field and those that are in the pipeline or contemplating careers in Arts Management, it's out of whack. But to the degree that we can increase participation by exposure, by hands-on experience, I think we can get more people engaged. It's important, also the audience, you can't think "Well if I put on *Porgy and Bess*, I'll get an audience." That may happen, but I also want the audience for Bill Bolcom's *View from the Bridge*. I want an audience for something else. That's why, for me, we have to be holistic about it. What role did arts education play in what I do? I can attribute what I do to the very early steps of the experiences that I achieved without hesitation.

In expounding on his proposition that the sector should think more holistically about addressing ADEI issues, Mr. Brown and I discussed arts education. I argued that the pipeline for building holistic participation in the arts is undermined by unequal access to arts education. Mr. Brown agreed, and offered this insight:

In the city of Detroit we've now gone over 30 years where arts education has not been a priority. There are isolated cases, yes, where there are specific schools that have terrific outcomes. But when we don't value that early exposure, involvement, participation, then it's very difficult to catch up. As it turns out, the newly appointed superintendent of schools part of his portfolio is that he was committed to arts and culture being part of a total education experience. The Detroit Symphony Orchestra, Michigan Opera Theater, Detroit Institute of Arts, have partnered to pilot a three-year initiative so all youngsters between grades of three and five will participate in a cultural passport. So we can recreate those kind of experiences like many of us had. My first exposure to an orchestra came about in the fourth grade, when I went to Ford Auditorium to hear the Detroit Symphony. Those hands-on experiences, we cannot underestimate the value they play long term. So what can we do to help turn that around? Have an intentional effort to look at something longer term. The investment we're making now that we agreed to over the next three years will not have a direct impact on the bottom line, the audiences we're serving today, a direct impact relative to being able to fuel the ranks of our employment needs. But it's starting a step that ultimately can re-engage more of our community to be able to take advantage of the art that we offer and that's where I believe we have to turn our attention.

He further discussed that he does not believe that the issue is one race or culture, but that it is an outcome of cities. He suggested that if the greatest diversity exists within urban centers, then the outcome is predictable. He continued:

That's why I believe that that exposure is not about creating more artists or managers, it's about opening the eyes and ears of our emerging generation to experience some of the things that I experienced. That can be, in my view, a factor if they want to become the head of an opera company, or if they want to be a trustee, if they want to be a staff member, if they want to practice law within the arts, that's where I think we can make a difference.

I agreed with Mr. Brown on this point. I also suggested that this is one of the places that more cultural organizations could have a bigger impact by committing to providing cultural experiences to K-12 students that communities can no longer expect from schools. However, too many cultural organizations shortsightedly would rather focus on performing or exhibiting without considering that investments in arts education ensures an audience for the performance or exhibition that they want to present (Rabkin & Hedberg, 2011). Furthermore, because of expenses associated with arts education, some cultural organizations have discontinued these critical programs altogether. Mr. Brown agreed with this point by saying:

> I hear it. And we've been through times of stress where the amount of time you devote to arts education is in competition with human resources, financial resources, but we have to be committed to it.

As we continued our discussion of arts education and its potential in holistically improving participation in the arts by many people, Mr. Brown shared a project that he worked on early in his career, by sharing this story:

> I remember the early part of my career with the Detroit Symphony, my charge was to create a tally of every orchestra. I remember reaching out, how many in Minnesota, how many in Baltimore, how many in Brooklyn, how many etc. etc. Therefore the Sphinx Organization has particular resonance for me because it was the first time a formalized effort was made to try to not only, it's not about head count, what kind of structure could be put in place to encourage putting more people in the pipeline. The organization aligning itself with a number of institutions, so it would be committed to hosting, engaging, and partnering. It resulted in what would have been a one and a half percent membership of symphony orchestras that were occupied by African Americans specifically, not just the issue of diversity, but African American, to as much as three to four percent following 11 years of operation with the Sphinx Organization. It may not seem a lot, the scale of orchestras in this country is huge, but it's been profound. The fact that we now have principal clarinettist in the Metropolitan Opera, we've got principal flute... I may be getting my instruments off, but brothers. Even within the last year, the steps that the League has taken in terms of its publications, it's being thoughtful, it's being mindful of optics, it's being the focus of making sure that at any given convening, what does the table look like? What does the room look like? Are we creating engaging moments for participants? All of that matters. OPERA America is beginning to do something of a similar nature.

As our interview began to come to a close Mr. Brown and I re-visited the discussion about mentoring, particularly as it relates to people of color who may desire to pursue a career in opera management. Making this connection is critical given that all of the respondents in this book had mentors who assisted them along their career paths, but only one actively and intentionally engaged in mentoring the next generation. Mr. Brown shared his view by stating the following:

> I think it's not just a conversation with a group of African American students alone. I think it's a conversation that can take place where African American artists or students are also present. Out of that, one can always have one-offs, but I'm not particularly interested in just having regular conversations with groups of African American students. I'm not opposed to it, but in terms of career development, I'd rather do that one on one, or I'd rather do that in a class that is diverse. One on one we can talk about particular skill sets and respond to particular needs. In a larger group we can talk about group dynamics, because it's important that not only are we talking together, but it's important that we have more David DiChieras in the room.

In closing, we re-visited the topic of progress related to racial ADEI in the U.S. cultural sector. I expressed my concern about the trauma that oppressed people experience in the cultural sector when the sector makes bold public statements about changing to create more spaces for those who have not been able to participate fully historically. In addition, to those who argue that the cultural sector has the same conversation cyclically every ten years without making any progress, Mr. Brown responded:

> Yeah, I would disagree. I would say I've seen significant change. Even with OPERA America. The conversation that took place about diversity in 2005, and conversations taking place now, worlds apart. That does not underscore the fact that there's so much to be done. I think the leadership role being played by OPERA America as being more that the leadership continues to evolve and therefore the leadership can tend to assert itself a little more. It's a different place. And that's a good thing. Sometimes those reactions are identical because one's experience tends to be contained and when it's contained you're going to have similar kinds of results. So one needs a little altitude. Sometimes all of us don't always allow ourselves to pull back a little bit.

References

Grensing-Pophal, L. (2018). *How to handle 5 generations in the workplace.* Accessed December 13, 2019. https://hrdailyadvisor.blr.com/2018/02/26/handle-5-generations-workplace/.

Rabkin, N., & Hedberg, E. C. (2011). *Arts education in America: What the declines mean for arts participation.* Accessed December 13, 2019. www.arts. gov/sites/default/files/2008-SPPA-ArtsLearning.pdf.

Sphinx Organization. (2020). *About. Sphinx.* Accessed December 13, 2019. www. sphinxmusic.org/.

5 Act IV: Michael Ching

From Composer to General/Artistic Director of Opera Memphis

Born on September 29, 1958 in Honolulu, Hawaii, Michael Ching was one year old when his family left Honolulu. This move afforded him the opportunity to grow up in New Orleans, Louisiana, and St. Paul, Minnesota. Because his grandparents were born in the United States, he described himself as a third-generation Asian American, one-quarter Chinese and one-quarter Japanese. He described his family as fitting the traditional cultural stereotypes about Asians as hardworking, wanting to become doctors, lawyers, or professionals of some sort.

At age six, he began studying piano, and at one point, he thought that he would become a concert pianist. Only later did he realize that the piano would also serve him well as a composer. In tenth grade, Interlochen School of the Arts in Michigan introduced him to composition during a summer camp. That summer, he discovered he had a facility for composing. He wrote a huge amount of music. His interest in music continued in high school. Mr. Ching's extracurricular activities all related to music. These activities plausibly impacted his career. In high school, he also saw his first full-length opera by Giuseppe Verdi. Although he does not remember which opera he saw, he does remember that the touring opera company gave a poor performance. He did not consider the schools he attended throughout his life diverse, but he did not think his race impacted his experiences.

Mr. Ching considered his father the family member who most influenced his career path. Though his father wanted to become a musician, the cultural milieu of his day did not allow it. But, Mr. Ching's father never discouraged him from becoming a musician. Mr. Ching's childhood was moderately disciplined, and although his family supported his interest in music, they wanted him to attend Duke as opposed to Eastman School of Music at the University of Rochester or the University of Michigan. He said, "They thought if I went to Duke, I would become a doctor." Although his mother did not complete her college education, his father earned master's and doctoral degrees and became a professor. Mr. Ching completed a B.A. in Music at Duke University. After his father passed, he did not believe that his mother thought negatively of his career pursuits. But, he and his mother had several conversations about his career decisions. He credited the Asian cultural values of hard work, discipline, and study as important to his development. He said, "I think it made me a little bit obsessed with having a regular paycheck, and so except for maybe two or three months of an essentially 25-year career, I have never not had a regular paycheck."

Mr. Ching assumed that most Asians succeed in the United States through assimilation (Lee & Kye, 2016). Because of this he knows very little Chinese and no Japanese. He shared this story:

They just couldn't understand why I wasn't interested in it. I am more interested in it now than I used to be, but the truth is that, you know, in our household, you'd have to look hard to figure out an Asian lives there; there are a few things, even here in my office. Feng Shui, I'm usually facing the door. There is a kind of Asian-looking teapot over there. I do drink tea. There is green tea in there. See, it is just one of those things that for me it actually hasn't been an issue.

He thought that the attitude towards assimilation has changed to one where Asians assimilate to a certain extent, but Asians also embrace certain cultural values and traits from their racial culture. He believed when and where you are raised plays a part in how you develop racially.

It surprised no one that Mr. Ching pursued a career in music. Immediately after graduating from Duke University he went into composing. As a composer, he found great compositional models in opera. Indeed, composition served as a useful route into the field of opera for him. In fact, his relationship with his composition teacher, Robert Ward, most influenced his career progression after college. Ward arranged his first job with Carlisle Floyd at the Houston Opera Studio and the National Opera Association. He expressed that currently there is a lack of mentorship in the field because no one wants to put her or his stamp of approval on the line. He said, "We tend to view helping someone else as not being in your best interest, but once you are in this field helping people is in your best interest." At age 21, Mr. Ching entered the field of opera, but every year until he was 30 or so he stated, "I would say, if I don't think this field is any good, I'll just get out of it and do something other than music." Mr. Ching ended up falling in love with it by doing it, but, he believed that he has a more ambivalent attitude towards opera than people who come into the field from different routes. Nevertheless, he is in opera for life.

He felt that it is important for arts administrators to figure out how they fit in. He said:

> Most of us go into the field of classical music to escape from the rest of the world, to narrow our focus. It is healthy because it makes you feel successful. It makes you feel like you have mastery of the world. But, it's not the world; we have to figure out how to relate to the world successfully so they won't ignore us.

His early exposure to opera reinforced his ambivalence because he was not sure that he would remain in the field as a composer or administrator. Nevertheless, his previous positions in opera included pianist and composer for the Houston Opera Studio, music administrator for the Florida Grand Opera, Music Director for the Triangle Opera Theatre, assistant to the General Director and associate Artistic Director at Virginia Opera, and General/Artistic Director of Opera Memphis. When I asked him about how he felt about diversity in executive opera management, he responded, "There is no diversity." But he did not regret his career choice. His experiences as a composer and administrator allowed him to take advantage of career opportunities he did not actively seek. These experiences came about because of the excellent career history he established in the field, first as a composer, then as an administrator.

Mr. Ching did not believe that his gender or race negatively affected his career. Nevertheless, he has experienced racism. He did believe that being born Asian can limit a person. But, he thought that people should not take incidents of racism too seriously. He said, "To me those kinds of things are more or less comical. It sort of depends on how you take those kinds of things. It might have been a little hurtful when you were eight, but it's something that you just can't take seriously." He shared this story:

> All three of the finalists/candidates for this job had wives. Statistically, this field is not run by heterosexuals, so something tells me that there was something going on that maybe was never written down on a piece of paper. So some things work for you and some things work against you. Statistically, if there are three finalists for a job as an Artistic Director you would think you would have at least one gay person.

Some opera companies in the United States have a bias for hiring certain types of opera managers. Mr. Ching said this: "Some companies only hire administrators from Europe. I can understand that in a limited dumb ass sort of way, but that's the attitude. It may be very subconscious."

Even though he has a mixed group of friends, he did not think his group of friends is mixed enough. But, Mr. Ching believed that living diversity is very important. When he first arrived in Memphis; he opened an account at the Black American-owned bank to establish a relationship. He said, "It was a way for me to make some kind of statement about diversity." He thinks the Asian population is large in classical music, so it is unremarkable that he is an executive-level opera manager. The color line he wants to break is the color line of becoming the first Asian to have a hit on country radio. That to him would be a cultural accomplishment because it would say something about the position of people of color in the United States. He shared this:

> Everyone assumes if you are Black, you are from here, unless you speak like you're from Jamaica, or the Caribbean, or some African country. They assume your family has roots here, but I can go somewhere and someone will think I just got off some boat. It annoys me because my family has been here for a long time.

He acknowledged that he is motivated by his own cultural baggage. Yet, he did not feel his appointment as General/Artistic director of Opera Memphis is entirely significant. He believed that holding the General/Artistic Director position as an Asian American is important in a global sense, but he does not consider it a cultural accomplishment.

Mr. Ching felt it is difficult to attract Asians to opera. Yet, when he lived in Memphis, the Asian community considered him one of its role models. He felt comfortable in this role, but because of the large number of African Americans in Memphis, he aimed to reach the African American community. He did not think that opera has solved the problem regarding attracting an African American audience. He shared this:

> It's so bloody obvious. The casting at Opera Memphis is very diverse and has been diverse, that has some positive impacts. That'll help get you to two or three percent. The answer is programming, but the problem is programming what? Why should that audience come, unless they get a piece every year? Then maybe they'll come to it and by the time you get them there for two or three years they've embraced the whole art form. The answer is programming, and it is so obvious.

He did not recall any opera company that has strategically programmed annually to target African Americans. He said, "No opera company has solved that problem. Basically, they all do *Porgy* or *Margaret Garner*. Well, and that's good. The Opera Company of Philadelphia seems sincere about it. They did *Margaret Garner* last year and they're doing *Porgy* this year, that's logical."

Regarding his career, he did not think he faced any barriers. He said, "My barriers are self-imposed. I admit that I would be farther along, if I wanted to." He also did not feel that his career path is any different from European American executive opera managers. When comparing the career paths of European American executive opera managers at level 3 companies across the country, similarities exist across career paths. The most significant difference is the entry into the field. As in the cases of the executives profiled in this book, some executive opera managers enter management from conducting, directing, managing, singing, or stage directing. Few enter the field from composition. Mr. Ching did not think affirmative action benefitted his career. He felt that affirmative action is mostly important in the early stages, such as access to higher education, so that all people of color are prepared to effectively compete with their European American colleagues.

Ten years from now, he wants to have had a number one hit on country radio. He also wants to contribute to solving the audience development problem relative to African Americans in opera. Still, Mr. Ching is happy and satisfied with his career path. He did not express an aspiration to work for an opera company higher than level 3. He shared this insight:

> My balance has more to do with the fact I work somewhere it's a perfect balance for me because there's enough, we look at the stuff we do and it can always be better. We have enough resources to do respectable work that the job is not so taxing that I can't go to Honolulu every summer.

The one expectation he did not have accepting his current position was dealing with full-time employees. In contrast to Linda Jackson's view that if an opera company wants to hire a diverse candidate they do not have to like opera, Mr. Ching discussed the difficulties in working with people who do not appreciate opera. He said, "You know the full-time employees that are the easiest to deal with are the ones who love opera." To a person of color aspiring to pursue a career in opera management or even Arts Management he said:

> It's a great opportunity. This field is wide open, whatever color you are, but especially for racially diverse managers. If you know what

you are doing, you will be very welcomed. It's hard to express: as a career option arts administration is just not up there. It's a hidden field, but you won't have any problems; it will provide you with certain kinds of opportunities.

Although Michael Ching did not consider himself a trailblazer, he felt that he is perceived as one because of his work in opera as a person of color. Mr. Ching currently serves as Music Director of Amarillo Opera, Composer-in-Residence at Savannah Voice Festival, and Opera consultant at EC Schirmer.

Reference

Lee, J., & Kye, S. (2016). Racialized assimilation of Asian Americans. *Annual Review of Sociology*, 42(2016), 253–273.

6 Act V: Linda Jackson

From Stage Manager to Managing Director of Connecticut Opera

Born on July 17, 1953, Linda Jackson grew up in the New York City metropolitan area. Ms. Jackson's earliest memory of opera occurred in sixth grade. Only after years of remembering spotty parts of a production that she saw, deducing that her teacher would not have taken her class to see something unpopular, and recalling that in the last act someone died in a bed, did she believe that Giuseppe Verdi's *La Traviata* may have been the first opera that she saw in middle school. However, she did not believe that this early exposure to opera had an influence on her career.

She described her family as supportive and upwardly mobile. Her father had a prestigious career in law and New York City politics, and her mother taught in the New York City public school system. Her brother worked as an attorney in the entertainment industry. Although not a big opera supporter, Ms. Jackson's mother avidly attends theater and dance. Ms. Jackson stated, "She goes to opera because I work in it." Her brother attends performances of opera. She said, "I made him be in an opera once down in Florida. He was obsessed with being on stage with Domingo. He enjoys it, but again, he is not a regular opera goer." Her father has also attended some of the shows that she has produced. As a result of her mother's interest in the arts, Ms. Jackson and her brother attended all kinds of shows growing up. She shared this story:

> I'm not sure why, but I ended up with a group of friends who put the shows on in high school. I think that contributed a lot to sort of how I got involved in this. Both my parents were very much into my brother and I pursuing professional careers and going to college and those kinds of things. It was up to us to decide where we wanted to go and what we wanted to do. In that sense it was a really supportive household and just not feeling like there was anything that we couldn't do.

When I asked her which family member most influenced her career path she responded, "Probably my mother in the sense that we went to the arts, but my father also because he taught me to be fearless."

Ms. Jackson has always had a mixed group of friends and associates, although she acknowledged that she has more White friends because of the field in which she works. Yet, Ms. Jackson has always had a comfort level relating with people of diverse racial backgrounds. This is something she believes she developed early on in her life. For example, because her mother taught, she attended high-achieving elementary, middle, and high schools. She shared this story:

> There was a book written in the 60s called Triumph in a White Suburb (Damerell, 1968), and it was about the movement of Blacks into a White community that was successful because the Whites technically didn't run. It was written about Teaneck, and that is where we moved. So from the time I was in the fourth grade until the time that I was a senior in high school in Teaneck, we were a very well-integrated community, very professional. I went to Bar Mitzvahs as well as Sweet 16s. All through high school kids were interracially dating. So we are talking in the 60s. My brother who is two years behind me actually started to experience the decay of that. So it was always very integrated, very mixed, we were all very collegebound, high achieving. You know, all my friends went to college, and we all sort of had aspirations toward professional careers

The extracurricular activity Ms. Jackson mostly participated in was church. But she also participated in a lot of after-school programs at the theater. I recognized a connection between her extracurricular activities and her career; she responded:

> It wasn't planned though. I went to high school like the usual. I went to college, and I was like, "Oh, I am not going to do shows for a while, I need to focus on my career." I had planned to be a doctor at one point, and then I got over that, and then I was going to be a lawyer. Then I planned to go to seminary. Then I got to college, and literally my freshman year dorm was across from the theater. I went over to volunteer and then just sort of after four years ended up being a theater major. It had not been my intent.

She double majored in English and Theater at Rutgers University, but she is not sure when she consciously decided to pursue a career in theater. She said, "Probably not until I was like into my Junior or Senior year. I knew that I wanted to go into theater, but I really wanted to go into straight theater. I thought it would be the coolest thing to be a Broadway stage manager. I wanted to produce at the Beaumont Theater."

While in college, Ms. Jackson shared that her mother repeatedly told her to get an education degree as a measure of security. Although her father always believed she should have gone to Law school, he encouraged her to do whatever she wanted to do as long it made her happy and successful. She also credits her father for helping her to develop a strong business sense. Her parents most influenced her career path by granting her permission to pursue the arts: "No one ever said, 'You shouldn't be doing that. Well, you know. There is no money in opera. Why don't you be a doctor?'"

At times, she thinks that her parents wonder how she got into opera because it is atypical. She said, "More than anything, they worry. We have a lot of conversations about fundraising and audiences and things like that, but I think they see that I am happy, and that is what is most important."

She identified her undergraduate department chairman as the person who most influenced her career decisions after graduation from high school and college. He taught her about production managing. After college, she immediately stage managed for one of her professors who had written a play. She and the professor became good friends, and for the next two years she worked on all of his productions. She said, "It sort of got me through my early stage in New York." She does not believe that her gender and race impacted her college experiences. She stated, "It was a very mixed program."

She identified her department chair at Rutgers and David Gockley at Houston Grand Opera as the mentors that most benefitted her career progression. She said, "I always had a really great relationship with David, and still a lot of what I know about producing opera and running a company, I learned from working with him. I still sometimes call him and ask him what he thinks." She also acknowledged the impact of working with Bob Herman in Miami. She said, "Bob ran a company in a very different way than David and with a very different artistic sense." She also identified Cynthia Auerbach at Chautauqua and Jane Weaver at the Texas Opera Theater program as mentors. Between these four mentors, Ms. Jackson learned the different ways she could manage an opera company; she stated:

> David is very much devoted to the art form and to exploring it and pushing its boundaries and not understanding boundaries. Bob was much more regimented and taught me a lot about discipline. From Cynthia I learned the undaunting belief that you cannot have an opera unless you have competent people who get along and function

as a group of people together. Interpersonal relationships within the staff are tantamount to having a successful company. Jane was also just very daring in terms of the way she just sort of put Texas Opera Theater together. We used to argue a lot, and that taught me a lot, too, because it helped me identify the things that I knew I did not want to do.

In our interview, Ms. Jackson identified first as a woman, second as a Christian, and third an African American. She shared this thought:

I am honestly glad I did not grow up White. It is not because I was necessarily a big, out-there, Black pro-whatever. It is just that I don't think I would have the opportunities or the sensitivity that I have if I had been raised as something comfortable. I mean I think the challenges that have been presented to me because I am a woman and because I am Black have made me a better person. I am not sure I would have had those same challenges if I had just been raised a White male, upper middle class, or something else. I am not sure I would have the same humility.

Ms. Jackson believes that race mattered to her family because of her father's involvement in New York City politics. She shared this story:

I did not consciously understand this until I was old enough. My father used to go down South and do a lot of voter registration. I never quite realized until I was an adult that on all those trips he was making he might not come home. That was really sort of eye-opening. It is interesting because this past Thanksgiving he was telling a story about being down in the South and being careful about how they went out and having police escorts. It was sort of scary. It was fascinating to hear but, very scary.

Yet, she does not feel she is on a mission. She stated, "I feel very strongly, and I feel it is very important for me to be successful at what I do because I have to continue to be in a position where I can be a role model." She also shared this story:

When I was at Chautauqua I was very conscious about how we handled colorblind casting and all of those issues. It is not as though I have gone out and done anything major or important in terms of wanting to change the nature of how the field works. For a short time actually, I worked at 651 at BAM (Brooklyn Academy of

Music). When I was hired there it was because Mickey Shepherd was running the organization and wanted to bring Opera Ebony in. Wayne and Ben just weren't interested. Part of me always wanted to work with a company that was African American, but part of it is having the resources to do it, and part of it is just trying to figure out where to do it. You know if I had been wealthy, I might have been able to start a company on my own but barring that it has been important to me to work in companies and organizations where I can make sure I can influence casting.

African American opera companies developed based on a similar philosophy to African American cultural organizations such as Alvin Ailey, Dance Theater of Harlem, True Colors Theatre Company, or any of the African American museums, essentially arts and culture about, by, for, and near Black people (Du Bois, 1926). These cultural organizations have audiences, boards, donors, and staff who are primarily people of color because they create a situation where those people are interested in those art forms. Ms. Jackson expounded on this:

> My parents knew one couple who are actually very big opera supporters. But they also go to see dance and financially support dance. I don't know if they would have supported dance had there not been places like Dance Theatre of Harlem and Alvin Ailey. Does that necessarily mean they have a different opinion of those art forms? No, there is still the fact that they are European classically based art forms that still sort of have no direct relationship to whatever the African American experience is. It is just that the nature of those companies has created a situation where people feel that there is an obligation to support them. Having a company like Opera Ebony would get support for the same reason. But just because say Willie and I are here; we are not necessarily going to generate a larger response from the African American community unless we were going to do a whole season of productions of operas geared towards African Americans. Even then I am not sure we would generate huge support because most people are just not into opera.

She also spoke about a discussion she had with a colleague about why Black people support African American opera companies:

> Opera Ebony used to have a relationship with a company in Philadelphia called Opera North. I remember having a conversation

with her once and she said, "What is frustrating to me about Opera North is that the productions are really bad, and as a result it is influencing the decision of Blacks to go to the opera." I said, "What are you saying?" She said, "Opera North will do a production of Marriage of Figaro, and they will sell lots of tickets, and they will have all these Black audience members there, but they don't go see productions at the Opera Company of Philadelphia or Pennsylvania Opera Theatre." I told her that they go because they see themselves reflected on the stage. It has nothing to do with the quality of the opera. They are not coming to see your shows because if there are all White singers up there, no one will be interested, and they won't care.

However, implementing colorblind casting racially is not always easy in opera because of personal aesthetic preferences (Mayo, 2018). But, Ms. Jackson shared this:

It's like if you watched television and you were an alien and you landed here and you turned on the television, you would believe that from watching commercials there was a comfortable ethnic mix in this country and that everybody is accepting of everybody else. You see a Black man and an Asian woman in their home doing the laundry. Part of the reason that I chose to stay in opera as a field originally was that the first time I did a production of *Butterfly* the soprano singing *Butterfly* was an African American. That was in a summer festival season, but then when HGO (Houston Grand Opera) did it on the main stage; we also had an African American in both casts. The first time I did *Butterfly* I thought there is something wonderful about this field where it does not matter as long as vocally the person is able to portray the role. The fact that was accepted made it much more interesting to me as a profession. It was also that I could get work in it. Now, that is not to say that there aren't all kinds of racial problems and inequities in the field, but it certainly is much more open and inviting.

Racially, Ms. Jackson defined herself as African American. I asked her, "why?" She responded, "Oh, I was saying that to be politically correct. I rarely use that term. I usually say Black because to me it is all words. It just makes me really crazy that in 2006 we are having this conversation anymore." When I asked her if there were times in her life being a person of color was more or less important to her, she stated:

> It becomes more important because society makes it more important. Therefore, becoming the first and only Black woman to run an opera company is important for that reason, which is stupid, as opposed to it just being important because I'm capable of running an opera company. That, of course, is important for that very reason, but that's a stupid reason. It is less important to me most of the time. Most of the time I just don't understand why it should be more important.

Yet, Ms. Jackson does believe she has experienced racism:

> I grew up in the 60s and 70s, and so it was more an issue because people were still very defined by their races. As a Black woman you become very conscious of the fact that you satisfy two stereotypical quotas when somebody is looking for you. I am sure I've had advantages I would not have had if I had been a Black man or a White woman.

She shared the following when speaking about the complexity of race in terms of work-related social activities:

> It is more about, you know, going to a cast party with a group of people who may or may not be prejudiced. It is not about, "Oh she's Black; she should not be stage managing." It is "Oh is it going to be okay to be at this person's home or something like that." You know, at first when I started in Houston, which was for better or worse, the South, and the same thing is true of Florida. You are a little bit conscious of that, but as time goes on and people get to know you and accept you, it goes away.

Ms. Jackson finds the sexist factor more prominent in the field. She said, "I very consciously feel, 'Oh, she could not possibly know what she is talking about. She is a girl.'" She has found this particularly in business communities involving boards, as she explained further:

> There are times when I feel like I bring it on myself. I know my voice pitches up when I am angry or excited or trying to make a point, and I wish it didn't. I would probably be better at that if I was a male, but I do think that there are times when I realize it would have been a lot easier to make the case if I was a guy in a business suit in a room with a bunch of businessmen.

For Ms. Jackson, it appears that her gender is more problematic than her race in opera. When I asked her about this, she expounded on the gender and race mix and its impact:

> I think it is different more than anything else. If I had been born ten years earlier and raised in Georgia, I am sure it would be very different than being born and raised in New York City and being part of a very prominent culture in Manhattan of upwardly mobile African Americans, Black Americans who were involved in politics. There were things that my father and mother were able to do that I know their parents weren't able to do. But I also know that because they were able to do it, they were not even issues for my brother and I. When I first went to Chautauqua as the production stage manager with Cynthia Auerbach, I remember when we first got there in the summer of 81, neither one of us would have been able to buy property at Chautauqua. No one would have sold to a Jew or a Black person; it would not have happened. I think the first Black family to buy a house there would have been maybe late 90s and Jewish property owners were probably a little bit earlier than that. I can remember laughing about the fact that the ladies running the opera company can't buy property. So again, a lot of things just naturally changed over the course of time. When you are in situations where you are surrounded by people who are more tolerant it's very different. The female thing I don't think has kept me from participating in things. I think that we are in a time where that would be politically incorrect. It is just a question of how much harder you have to work to make an impact.

When discussing bi-cultural competence and the challenges negotiating racial identities in a White-dominated world, Ms. Jackson stated:

> I'm not any different. I feel like a few people can't figure out why I work in opera. It's not because it is White; it is because it's opera. I get that more than I get working in a European environment. But I never felt like I had to change to adapt to either of those situations in any way.

I asked Ms. Jackson if she thought it was easy or more difficult to attract Black Americans to opera; she responded:

> I am assuming we are hearing from more singers of color than a lot of other places are in terms of wanting to audition for us and

everything, which is sort of a blessing and a curse, because I think there is also some expectation that we are going to be more accepting. A bad singer is a bad singer no matter what color they are. You know, it is sort of an awkward kind of position to be in. We certainly both get asked for advice from singers about career and what they want to do and what our experiences have been. This does not happen as much here because Willie is such a prominent figure here. Certainly more people who don't know anything about the field know about Willie as being out there, than necessarily know about me. It was a bit different when I was at Chautauqua, but when I was General Director, I used to get that a lot. Unfortunately, it does get taken a step further, which is to say that I think there are singers who think, "I have a better shot at getting hired because both Willie and Linda are Black." And that is an unfortunate belief, because like I said, if you can't sing, you can't sing.

When I asked Ms. Jackson about her feelings regarding diversity in opera management at the executive level, she responded, "It doesn't exist." She explained:

> Well, but there is a reason it doesn't exist. Why would you choose to go into opera? First of all, let's say you are White. Why would you choose to go work for an opera company? Unless you were predisposed for some reason, it has such a minority support anyway. It's such a small niche of people that are responding to opera versus the whole rest of the entertainment field to begin with. So next, well, suppose you are Black, Latino, or Asian or anything like that. If you take a look, and I don't know if anyone has done this, I always thought we should. If we look at the percentage of people of color that are involved in opera as an art form on a percentage basis and apply that to whatever is the percentage base of the population that you are talking to. It's probably the same percentage; it just looks different because you don't see so many minorities. But, the reality is that there are not a lot of people there to begin with.

Ms. Jackson further expressed her frustration at the field's response to diversity employment recruitment and retention by sharing these thoughts:

> During my years on the board of OPERA America, we would have a lot of discussions about diversity at opera companies. It would come up. Well, we have a hard time finding good singers of color who have been trained, particularly Blacks. I think that is true. I think

that the ability to be able to financially afford what you need to do is very difficult on young African Americans. It's hard on White singers, too. They would say, "What are we going to do?" I would say things like, "You know, you don't have to just hire Black singers. You can hire a Black receptionist. You don't have to like opera to be a receptionist. You don't have to like opera to be a finance director. It's a job."

Ms. Jackson thinks affirmative action is important because the problem that the government intended to solve still exists. She made this point:

Part of where affirmative action has failed is less on the part of people who are the decision makers as much as it is on the people who need to go forward. I think we have done enough education with minorities to be able to say you need to be pushing yourself more. That is where the shortfall has come is that affirmative action has spent a lot of time rewarding people for doing stuff that they really should have pushed themselves a little bit more to do on their own. And I am not a person who believes we should get rid of affirmative action. I just think that it is important to make sure people understand what the goals are in all that.

Still, Ms. Jackson does not think affirmative action benefitted her career progression in Arts Management. She said:

You know, I don't believe it has. I mean affirmative action did not benefit my career. It affected my start. Like I said before, because my father and his generation had positions and created experiences, it made it that much easier for my generation to be successful. Hopefully, my generation has made it that much easier to be successful for someone else.

Although she does not think race factors into succeeding as an opera manager, she wondered if opera as a field by virtue of what it is has the potential to attract different races. Ms. Jackson spoke about this more:

More than just opera being a European art form is working against it. There is no money. It is expensive. It is not for profit. It is hard to make a living. It's not the same kind of money. Given the kind of work I do here, if I was working for a corporation I would be making three times as much money, but I don't think there are barriers necessarily in terms of administration. I just think it is not a choice that people are going to make. There are not White people making the choice at this point, either. There is going to be a void soon if we don't address how to deal with it. It is about compensation packages, and some of it is about just the workload and support systems that there are for nonprofit.

Ms. Jackson does, however, think gender comes into play to some extent. She also talked more about the issue of her race:

> I can't say definitively that it does not. I interviewed for Orlando once upon a time. There were many factors that I think contributed to me not being considered seriously. I think my race was part of it because it was Florida, but I also know it was because I was a woman. I also know it was because I was single and didn't have a family. I think I was just the wrong fit. You know it is interesting. When you go through an interview process, you are interviewing companies as well as they are interviewing you. You are more successful if it is as attractive to you. You present yourself better. In all the instances there were places where I did that. Like do I wish I had gone to Orlando Opera? I'm glad I didn't go to Orlando Opera. So as a result I think you sort of influence the decision that people are making as well. I also think it has something to do with how you present yourself and whether or not it is the right mix or not. I'd like to believe at this point in time, particularly in a nonprofit, that the right mix won't be trumped by somebody's race or sex. I have to believe that at this point in time, because I think that bears out more often than it doesn't.

In terms of looking at how cultural organizations view balancing diversity issues with grant funding agencies' desires, she does not think it really matters if a person is into opera or not. She said, "We are talking about basic office jobs that have to be filled. Now this gets back to, it still has to be a choice. I am not sure that if someone of color were to look through the want ads, because I had advertised for a receptionist they might necessarily say, 'Well, I am going to go there because it's an opera company.' You know, that's different."

Ms. Jackson also spoke about working with the Brooklyn Academy of Music (BAM). Because there is an emphasis on hiring from the Brooklyn community, the staff is naturally much more diverse. She said:

> Working at BAM is like being at the UN. You know, the first time I went to the Christmas party, I mean everybody was there.

The head of the finance program at BAM when I was there was Black. Her assistant was Asian. The rest of the staff was like Black or Latino. It was like the Rainbow Coalition working at BAM because they hired out of the community.

She thinks most performing art forms are bad about hiring people who are not passionate and interested in the art form. She said:

It never occurs to anybody that the receptionist does not have to love opera to answer the phone. I think that tends to be what happens a lot. Part of that comes because we don't pay as well as a lot of other people. The assumption is that you are going to look for somebody who wants to work there.

She does not believe that active discrimination is the cause for the lack of diversity among executive opera managers. She said, "Opera is a conscious choice. It is not like when you are growing up Black, somebody says, 'Don't forget to think about working for an opera company.'"

Ms. Jackson had very little management preparation, but she shared this:

I started as a stage manager and had a full theater training background and pretty much stage managed. I guess it was in Houston when I realized that stage managers sort of have to know everything. A stage manager is in on pretty much every decision that has to be made. I am a natural organizer, and all of that, so it was an easy enough transition into being a production manager because when you are a production manager you are managing budgets, and it was easy enough to develop an understanding of the budget and budgeting and all of that. There wasn't any formal training. I didn't do a degree in Arts Management or that type of thing.

Yet, stage managing serendipitously assisted her in becoming a leader. She had always been a production manager. She never intended to become the head of an opera company, but she shared this thought about how it happened for her, "Literally, I was number two, my boss died, and they promoted me. You know, Chautauqua is a unique experience because you are not directly responsible for your fundraising, so it was easy enough to run a company without having to have that part. I don't know, it just happened." None of her training directly dealt with diversity; she said:

I assume that when you are working you hire people that you have some personal evaluation skills to be able to tell if somebody is a good person or not. I believe that people are basically honest and hardworking, and if you tell me that you can do something, we will hire you to do it. If you can't then we fire you.

When I asked her how her knowledge of management principles assisted her in gaining her current position, she responded, "I don't think it is knowledge. To me it's logic." She explained the difference:

I mean there is nothing formal about it for me. The nature of Chautauqua every summer and the staffing there. It can't apply here because I have the same staff here, but the staffing at Chautauqua changed every summer. The composition of the staff, it was like if I hired a stage manager who had these types of skills, then I knew when I was hiring the other stage manager that I had to look for someone who had a different type of skill. Depending on the stage managers, how that was going to affect the company. I always hired personalities. I have always hired people that I knew were going to get along with each other. I would rather hire a person who has really good ethics and morals, but perhaps not the best skill set because I believe skills can be taught if someone is intelligent. I would rather know that people are going to get along. It is just sort of instinctual because that is the way I want to work. I want to work with people who laugh a lot, who have a good time, who have a great sense of humor, but who also are going to get the work done. But, I mean I don't think that happened as a result of any type of formal training. It was a result of working with all of these different people. I mean for as serious as David Gockley is, I have seen a side of him and a sense of humor that I absolutely adore. Bob Herman was a very, very stern person and was sort of formidable in some ways, but still was accessible. Cynthia was really into having a big family, and Jane was really into having a big family. But, it wasn't any sort of formal training.

Ms. Jackson received her first job in opera as a stage manager. Her first job in opera management came about because Chautauqua needed a production manager. She spoke about the occurrence of career opportunities not sought, but gained through serendipity's intervention:

I was in the Assistant Managing Director position, which put me in charge of everything when Cynthia (Auerbach) found out she had lung cancer. She died two months before the season started. At that point, everything was in play, so they just decided not to bring anybody in at that point. We just let the season run, and at the end of the season they said, "Well, you know what you are doing." I didn't have any choice. I mean I was Production Manager in Houston, and I was sort of Managing Director at Chautauqua, and Cynthia died. Then they asked me to be General Director. Then suddenly I was a General Director.

Chronologically, Ms. Jackson's career has included positions as stage manager, production manager, Managing Director, and General Director. She stage managed in Houston and Miami, stage managed and production managed at Chautauqua, then became Managing Director and General Director at Chautauqua, also General Director for the Berkshires Opera Company. She held positions with the Byrd Hoffman Foundation/Watermill Center, Opera Pacific, New York City National Opera Company, and the Brooklyn Academy of Music. I asked Ms. Jackson, knowing what she knows now, what changes would she have made in the course of her career path. She shared this insight about the importance of recognizing career opportunities not sought:

> None of it was choice. I am in New York; my friend calls me and says I need an assistant for three months. What are you doing? I told him I didn't know anything about opera. He says you know how to stage manage, come to Houston. I went to Houston for three months. It was supposed to be three months. Got to Houston and stayed through Spring Opera Festival, and they asked me to come back the next year. I ended up staying there for three years. I only got to the point where at the end of that time I was ready to go back to New York and do theater again. So I moved back to Boston with my boyfriend and thought I would go back and pursue my career there. Got another phone call from another friend of mine, the same person, who was now in Washington. He needed an assistant. So I went there. Another friend called and said, "I am going to be in Miami in the spring. Can you come down and help me?" I told him sure, no problem. We were in the house one day, and the phone rings. Cynthia called my friend and said, "I am going to Chautauqua Opera. Will you come stage manage for me?" My friend said, "No, I am going to Santa Fe. But wait a minute let me give the phone to Linda." Cynthia was looking for a stage manager. I did not know her, and I went to Chautauqua. I mean that is what happened.

Ms. Jackson's career also advanced because of a formal and informal social network that worked for her serendipitously. She further explained:

> Yes, but no choices, and even going from Chautauqua to BAM, even that, Mickey wanted to bring Opera Ebony to Brooklyn. She asked if there were any Black opera administrators out there; she did not know anything about opera. She called me and said she needed an opera administrator there. You know there was no point where I consciously said I wanted to do this. It has sort of been a natural progression of things. And a couple of times I have actually thought about pursuing other companies or interviewing, but I wasn't hired.

Ms. Jackson and I discussed that in U.S. society it seems that the people who pursue success are the ones who succeed. The idea of letting it happen and preparing to respond to unsought career opportunities caused me to reconsider my own career strategies. She said:

> It is a little scarier that way. Ninety percent of my jobs started with me. Like the position in Houston, I was the first person to hold that. I mean, you know the stage-managing thing pretty much, but when I went to BAM that position started with me. I can think of some other things that started with me.

I asked Ms. Jackson about the personal and professional qualities that caused Connecticut Opera to select her for her current position, She stated, "Well, I think part of coming here is the fact that I knew Willie, so that had a big influence on it. Then well, you know, the rest of it just spoke for itself." She did not experience any major challenges in the application and interview process. But, the realities of serving in an executive opera manager's position are more difficult than she anticipated. She stated, "I just thought it wouldn't be quite so hard. It is harder than I thought. It is hard to bring a company together. It is hard managing." When I asked her about barriers to her career success, she shared this insight:

> I don't know that I had any barriers. I know that there are continuing barriers, like you are always dealing with a board that is not always what you want them to be. You are always dealing with not having enough money to do the things that you want to do. I don't know that there has ever been anything that I felt kept me from doing what I wanted to do. I just think I am one of those people

who just aren't receptive. I definitely don't think the barriers are necessarily about the color issue. Because of the places I have worked. Even being a woman, that is really anecdotal in having to deal with specific people just not paying attention to you.

The career strategy Ms. Jackson used to work through feeling like certain colleagues were not listening to her defined perseverance; she said:

You just keep doing it. I figure sooner or later they are going to get it or not. You know, you can spend a lot more time trying to explain things and justify things, although I am not sure that is really bad because it does really force me to re-think things. It really does just sort of force you to look at things differently, but when you are dealing with people who aren't listening the first time, you find different ways to look at everything, and in the process you refine and make the arguments better for yourself.

Ms. Jackson thinks the most difficult issue she has faced in her career as a person of color or woman is getting people to understand what she is talking about; she relayed this point:

I am never sure if I am not explaining it well or if it is because people don't hear what I am saying. It becomes so very clear for me, that and I can be so focused on what I am talking about that I just lose sight of whether I am being clear. It is not until I am running up against people who just don't completely understand what I am trying to say. I don't know that it is emotional or psychological. I mean, to me the most difficult thing is trying to create art in a society where it's not a priority, and it has nothing to do with race or sex or anything. We are dealing with the United States where these are not priorities, and it is very difficult to continue functioning when you are struggling and are constantly at the mercy of everybody else in order to survive.

Despite the difficulty of creating a safe space for an unpopular art form to thrive, Ms. Jackson is still committed to opera. When I asked her if she would choose opera management if she had to make her initial career decision again, she stated:

It really was not an initial career decision. I like it a lot, and I don't regret it. Would I have initially made that choice? I don't know. Probably not. I don't know what I would have done differently because it just sort of happened. I was happy with that. It was not like this was the area I want to go in.

The most significant incident that impacted Ms. Jackson's professional development was the death of her supervisor at Chautauqua Opera. She said, "Even at the point when I was her Managing Director it did not occur to me that I would run the company. I just assumed that I would be in the number two position, so probably that is the most significant thing that happened and made a difference for me." This incident taught her that she knew a lot more about opera than she thought she did:

> I figured out that I knew more about producing opera. I didn't study opera, and so when I started working at HGO as a stage manager it was sort of learning on my feet. In terms of the ability to learn and manage an organization, I mean, I guess I sort of realized I did know how to do it. I still feel like I am learning a lot about it all the time, but I guess certainly I realized that it was a skill set and an ability that I had all the time and it seemed to suit me okay.

Ms. Jackson expressed that her career path is similar to that of White executive opera managers. She also believes that most executive opera managers of her generation were singers, directors, or conductors:

> There were no Arts Administration programs like there are now. You know, people were singers, or they were directors, or they were conductors, and they were not necessarily successful in those areas, but they had a good business background, and they became the General Director. Now it is very different. They go to school, and they think, "Oh gee, I might want to run an opera company," and they take the courses, and they go do it. But in our time, it just was not the way it happened.

When I asked Ms. Jackson if she thought she would have studied Arts Management had there been programs during her collegiate years, she responded:

> Probably not, because I really loved the process of being on stage and in production so at that point in my career when I was in college I would have probably been leaning towards wanting to be a stage manager or something like that. It would've never occurred to me then to work in opera. I really think too, because when I started working in opera as a stage manager, companies weren't hiring

stage managers for opera. You would see if there was somebody local, and there were a few of us out there who really were stage managers who were doing it. That is very different now, too. Across the board there is more professional training in terms of all the positions in opera than there were when I started, which was 30 years ago. When I was in college it never would have occurred to me to actually think that long term I would be doing administrative work.

Although Ms. Jackson is not currently mentoring anyone, she maintains that stage managing is the best way to learn opera management. She provided this advice for an executive opera manager aspirant:

If you can be at a company where it is really hands-on, you can really understand how the shows go together, and it will also help you figure out whether or not you can deal with people. If you can deal with artists and artists' egos and all of that, then you have a better shot at being a good administrator long term, whether it is opera or any place for that matter. The rest of it just sort of depends on your intuition and your instincts. Part of it overall is just dealing with people.

Ten years from now, Ms. Jackson still wants to produce operas. But she thinks the bigger problem is if she can continue her work because of attitudes about the arts:

I saw a production of *Atys*. It was the closest thing to perfect that I have ever seen, and I have yet to produce mine. I have done some productions that I am really happy with. I can look at about five different things that I have been associated with in my career, and every time I do a new one it bumps something off the list, but I still don't feel that I have done one where I can definitively say like, "that's the best work I have ever done." I know I will strive for that for the rest of my life because that is what I want to be able to do.

Turn of the Screw at the Berkshires, *Giovanni, Trilogy, Don Pasquale*, and *Cosí* are the five productions Ms. Jackson is most proud of throughout her career.

Ms. Jackson and I discussed nonprofits further. We both agreed that nonprofits do not do a good job marketing themselves as career options. Yet, if nonprofits expect to recruit and retain good managers of color, it will become increasingly important for them to package the idea of "making a contribution to society" so that it is more appealing work, given the low salaries and non-existent work/life balance. Ms. Jackson shared more:

> There are realities about it. You know, you go from college where you are thrown in with a group of people who are doing all different things from all walks of life. So there you are ten years from now, and you are working for American Red Cross and you are making $35,000 a year, but ten years from now your roommate who decided to be a lawyer is making $400,000 a year. I mean there is a certain amount of that. I think we are better at it and I think that people want to do it, but then there are also the realities of whether or not you can survive or not.

When I asked Ms. Jackson why she thought people of color should pursue careers in executive opera management, she responded:

> Why not? Why would anybody not pursue a career in opera if they are interested? From an administrative point of view, I don't see that there are barriers. Now maybe I am being naïve, and Willie may have a different opinion about that, but I don't think so. But, finding African Americans that want to do it.

She advises people of color who want to become executive opera managers to question their desire. She feels that her work is so difficult that she is wondering if it can be fun anymore. Dealing with a non-sympathetic public is difficult because it relates to funding in the country. Also, a great deal of competition exists for entertainment venues. She shared this insight:

> I would say that if it is about wanting to be an executive director in an arts organization that is one thing. If it is about wanting to be an executive director of an opera company, then I would say that you have got to be sure that is really what you want to do because it is not going to be easy for you to be successful because the job is not going to be easy.

Over her more than 30-year career in the field, Ms. Jackson most frequently mentioned funding, the costs to produce opera, arts education, popular cultural trends, programming repertoire that can compete with or complement current movie trends, and limited repertoire as the most challenging trends to observe in opera management. In terms of academic training or leadership development relative to encouraging people of color to pursue a career path in opera management, Ms. Jackson said this:

> A lot of it has to do with the field being successful and people deciding to choose it as an option. The problem, in terms of educa-tion, I think there needs to be better education about the arts in general, and not just about creating executive directors for a busi-ness. It is about creating corporate executives who understand that they need to be philanthropic at the same time. I think it is about general arts education awareness across the board for everybody whether they end up pursuing a career in the arts or not.

Ms. Jackson thinks that in her youth that she took more risks. When it comes to management, however, she thinks people become more con-servative and cautious as they age. She spoke about how her responsi-bilities at Chautauqua allowed her to take a lot of risks because she was not responsible for fundraising:

> They just gave me my budget, and I could go with it. So it is a lot easier to be a lot bolder than when you are sort of having to raise money or anything. In other situations, you start to second-guess yourself.

She does not consider herself a trailblazer, but she does consider herself a student of everything:

> I'm really good at looking at something and saying that I want to try it and perhaps figuring out a way to do it better and continue it, as opposed to coming up with a brand-new idea and taking it for-ward. If I see somebody do something at another company, I might try it here, but I might try this variation, and it might move it that much further along.

I explained to Ms. Jackson that the question came from looking at her career and bio and thinking that her career has gone in a different direction than what is generally expected from a Black woman. She said, "Probably from 100 feet out there, yeah. But from way up here it is kind of like, you know, it just kind of happened." Ms. Jackson shared this last insight:

> It wasn't choice. It happened. It worked out. I really love it. Would I have done it again? I don't know. I might have made different

choices. I look at things. Should I have done film training; maybe. I look at the field and I think I don't know how they survive in the movie business. It is all cutthroat. I used to work part-time for my brother. The recording industry makes me sick. It is very cutthroat. So you know, I mean, nonprofit was where I was probably supposed to end up. I like producing. I like making shows. I like creating entertainment for people, but you know. I don't want to say I've been lazy, but it all sort of happened and as a result of things happening it has allowed me to be a little bit bolder about making some choices. Ultimately, it wasn't my choice. It wasn't like I said this is where I want to go. I think that has made it more interesting because it wasn't on a path. My ideal cross-country trip would be to drive cross country and to stop and read markers and then say, "Oh, gosh, look there is something down here," and be able to go off and know that I had the year to do it.

Linda Jackson currently serves as Managing Director of Byrd Hoffman Water Mill Foundation.

References

Damerell, R. (1968). *Triumph in a White suburb: The dramatic story of Teaneck, N. J., the first town in the nation to vote for integrated schools.* William Morrow.

Du Bois, W. E. B. (1926). Krigwa Players Little Negro Theatre. *Crisis,* 32(1926), 134.

Mayo, L. (2018). *Color blind casting is a step forward for no one.* Accessed December 13, 2019. https://studybreaks.com/news-politics/color-blind-casting/.

7 Act VI: Willie Anthony Waters

From Conductor to General/Artistic Director of Connecticut Opera

Born on October 11, 1951, Willie Anthony Waters grew up in a town south of Miami, Florida. Everybody in his family sang. At four years old, his grandmother began teaching him how to read music and play piano. Once old enough, he accompanied a family singing group on the piano that toured various churches and other organizations in Florida. Both of his parents completed high school, and his father completed two years at Florida Agricultural and Mechanical University (FAMU) in Tallahassee, Florida. His father worked as a shipping and receiving clerk for Harrell & Kendall Company, at one time the largest producer of fresh fruit in South Florida. His mother, a housewife, owned a beauty parlor that she ran on their back porch. Maestro Waters' oldest brother and sister studied operatic singing, which is where he first received exposure to the art form. Another of Maestro Waters' brothers played trumpet and minored in trumpet in college. Clearly, Maestro Waters' family immersed him in music at a very early age.

Various family members influenced Maestro Waters' career, including the three siblings mentioned earlier, two of whom attended FAMU. He also believes that another brother who served in the Vietnam War also influenced him. This particular brother joined a record club and would periodically send Maestro Waters operatic recordings. In addition, he credits his grandmother with pushing him to read and play music, and to learn repertoire. Although he does not believe that his family understands how he chose a career path that led him into opera, Maestro Waters' family supported his career in opera, particularly when he became Artistic Director of the Greater Miami Opera. He shared:

> They all came in mass for the first couple of years. My oldest sister, of course, was very interested. My mother would always go and drag a couple of my aunts along with her. My two younger sisters, initially, would go, because it was an exciting thing for them to see

their brother up there conducting an opera. So they all appreciated it. My oldest sister and brother knew more about it than the others did, so they would go even when some of the others wouldn't. Initially, they all went and dragged my little nieces and nephews along. One of my nieces went to a couple of opera performances last year. She said, "It was because of the experience I had when you were there conducting, so I really got to like it."

When I asked Maestro Waters about his earliest memory of opera, he responded:

My earliest memory of opera is when my sister sang the "Inflammatus" from Rossini's *Stabat Mater*. Our high school chorus presented it, and she was the soprano soloist. I was sort of knocked away because of the high C's at the end. I thought, Whoa! Then her last year at FAMU in 1962 we all drove up for her graduation. The chorus, Rebecca Steel was the choir director then, did the "Halleluiah" from King of Kings with band. Even though it's not opera, it was very operatic, and that sort of knocked me away.

These early experiences with operatic music proved powerful for him. But, he also shared more about other early exposures to opera that he received in childhood:

The *Ed Sullivan* show was on television, and there were always opera singers on *Ed Sullivan*. The first one I remember hearing was Roberta Peters, and then Richard Tucker, and then Leontyne Price. That started around ninth grade.

In tenth grade, Maestro Waters played trumpet in his high school marching band. The band director introduced his students to opera through recordings and performance by programming the "Triumphant scene" from Verdi's *Aïda*. He spoke about this more:

He said, "Now, I want you to hear it the way it really should be with all the voices and orchestral instruments." Again, I was sort of knocked out. There is just something that just spoke to me in a way that nothing had up to that point. That was in the early spring of that year. I ended up having a free period later towards the end of the school year. I asked him if I could come into the band room and learn some of this music and listen to some of this music. He said sure, and he bought a couple of more recordings. I would sit with the libretto, and I had no idea of Italian or any of that kind of stuff, but I was particularly interested in the *Aïda*.

The operatic recording of *Aïda* starring Leontyne Price made a lasting impression on Maestro Waters. His band director encouraged him to listen to the entire recordings:

> I got so hooked. I was doing it day in and day out. The other two recordings were *Lucia di Lammermoor* with Roberta Peters and *Don Giovanni* with Sutherland. I wasn't nearly as interested in those because they did not have Leontyne. The fact that she was a Black singer doing this, I would go to the library and read up on everything that I could about her, and it just made such an impression. I guess that sort of planted the seed deep down inside.

The following year, Maestro Waters joined the Upward Bound Program at the University of Miami (UM). Through this program, he had access to UM libraries. His band teacher once again encouraged him to take advantage of all the music at his disposal:

> My band teacher who introduced me to those recordings said, "You have the music library there. Why don't you start listening to various operas?" He gave me a list of the most popular operas, which were those three and *Don Giovanni, La Bohème*, and said in your spare time just go and start listening. I had afternoons off during the summer, so I would go, and I would sit for hours and just start listening to these recordings.

By the time he graduated from high school, he considered himself totally immersed in opera.

Throughout the tenure of his education, Maestro Waters primarily attended predominantly Black schools. However, in eleventh grade he had his first White teacher. She taught Biology and loved opera. She took five honors students, including Maestro Waters, to live performances of ballet, symphonies, and opera. He shared this story:

> She bought the tickets and everything, that was around 1967, and that was when I saw my first live opera performance, which was *Madame Butterfly*. Irene Patti Schwartz sang the role of Butterfly. She was a principal singer of the Miami Opera, the Florida Grand Opera now, and she is also a distant relative of Adelina Patti. Later we talked more about all of that, and I said to her that she was very

much responsible for me being in opera because of that first experience. Seeing Butterfly on stage was just amazing.

This early exposure to opera was crucial to Maestro Waters' career path
and success. His career aspirations, plans, and goals before college were
to become a concert pianist, but he tired of practicing and grew more
interested in opera. He gave up studying applied piano and decided to
major in music education. He said, "That seemed to be the safest thing.
There are loads of teachers in my family, and my mother said that you
need something that you can fall back on and that typical kind of thing,
so I went with education." After changing his major in his second year,
he concentrated on accompanying and opera. He also became involved
with UM's opera workshop. The opera coach saw his interest in opera
and asked him if he wanted to help with the program. Although he did
not seek out this opportunity, it proved beneficial. He shared this story:

> She asked if I would like to be involved as a go-for. She let me assist
> her, and I played some rehearsals, not very many because my chops
> were not so great at that time. Just being in the environment, that
> was really exciting and really interesting. When I entered the Uni-
> versity of Miami in September, she was saying you ought to stay
> involved in the opera workshop. Then she died that year, and the
> whole situation with the opera workshop was in flux.

Music education majors study all musical instruments. As a result,
Maestro Waters studied voice as a part of his degree. Ironically, his voice
teacher, Mary Henderson Buckley, was the wife of Emerson Buckley,
who at one time in his career served as the Artistic Director of Greater
Miami Opera. Mrs. Buckley encouraged him to work with the opera
workshop and to conduct opera scenes. Mrs. Buckley also introduced
him to her husband, who then invited him to audition for the Greater
Miami Opera chorus. He relayed this:

> I was not a singer, but I could sing, and I was studying with her,
> and I was a good enough musician, so they took me into the chorus.
> That next summer, the opera company got a grant to do opera
> excerpts in parks. The county had a mobile show, and they would
> do performances on this portable stage. They decided five of those
> performances they wanted to do as opera. It just so happens that
> two of the places they wanted to perform were Liberty City, and the
> other was Richmond Heights, where I grew up. They did some PR
> and everything on the fact that I was from that area. We had huge

crowds, and that was my first experience doing something like that. I even narrated. A lot of my friends came from high school. That was my first exposure to that kind of live performance. We did cut-down versions of *Bohème* and *Butterfly*. I would prepare and play the piano for the performances.

After graduating from UM, Maestro Waters decided to attend graduate school to study conducting. He auditioned for three schools: Manhattan School of Music, the Conservatory of Music at the University of Cincinnati, but he could not remember the other school. Manhattan School of Music rejected him because he had little to no conducting experience. Both Cincinnati and the other school accepted him. Cincinnati offered him half of an assistantship and other assistance. This opportunity excited him because he would study with Thomas Schippers, one of Leontyne Price's principal conductors. Later, he learned that Mr. Schippers engagements kept him away from school, but he shared this:

Out of the clear blue sky I walked into the University of Miami School of Music and looked on the bulletin board, and there is an announcement from Memphis State University for a new program in operatic coaching and conducting, which would be run by George Osborne. The person in charge of the actual participants would be Kip Cutchstedder, Mignon Dunn's husband. I applied, the next week George called and asked if I would come to Memphis for an interview and audition. They flew me to Memphis, and I went, auditioned, and he offered me the job on the spot. It was a new program, half-sponsored by the state, half-sponsored by the university. I didn't have to put any money into it. It was a complete free ride. I said, "Why not?"

Maestro Waters planned to start his graduate studies in September, but his plans changed quickly:

In the latter part of June, George called and said I just fired my pianist. We are doing two shows this summer, *Purlie* and *South Pacific*, and I just want to know if you would be available and interested in coming. I said, "Okay, when?" He said next week. I said, "Okay." I quit the job that I was going to have for the summer, and I moved to Memphis towards the end of June and stayed there. I went there, I arrived about 4:00 in the afternoon, and there was a chorus rehearsal of *Purlie*, a piece I had never heard, and I had never seen a piece of the music or anything, and I had to do the rehearsal. I said, "You know this is putting me in a very precarious position." He said, "Well, from what I understand, you are a very good musician."

This experience demonstrated his ability to courageously respond to serendipity. It also showed his amazing will to succeed artistically under pressure:

George decided he was only going to conduct the opening night. Then he was going to turn it over to me, but he never told me that. I had only conducted a string quartet at that point. Even though *Purlie* is not a huge orchestra, there were about 15 people in the band. I went through the last couple of rehearsals and the opening night, and then he said, "Okay, it's yours." It was a musical so it was not so bad, but I was frightened. But, it worked. My two years at Memphis State gave me the opportunity to work with the student orchestra. I was in front of the orchestra practically at least once or twice a week for the whole two years I was there. That's the way it is. That is the way you learn. You can't sit in the practice room. You get some of the basics there, but you have to do it. You just have to get in front of the band and do it.

Maestro Waters, however, had concerns about Memphis because of Dr. Martin Luther King Jr.'s assassination there. Nonetheless, Maestro Waters' decision to attend Memphis State proved one of the best things he ever did in his career. Yet, challenges existed. The first year of the program, he was the only Black graduate student in the School of Music. He said, "Being a Black graduate student in a program like that involving opera is very unusual. There were just all kinds of crazy thoughts that were going through my mind." Maestro Water's concerns are not unfounded. Even today, African Americans make up a little over 10% of those enrolled in graduate programs in the U.S. (Okahana & Zhou, 2019). As a relatively unstructured program, Memphis Opera Theater at Memphis State University needed an accompanist, too. This joint community effort with the opera company and the university provided students with several performance and managerial opportunities.

I asked Maestro Waters, "How important was race to his family?" He answered, "I don't know that it was. I don't remember there being a conversation, 'You must do this because you're Black, or you must do this because there are no African Americans.' It was only you must go where your goals and talents takes you." Maestro Waters also spoke about his mentors, Mrs. and Dr. Buckley at UM, never discouraging his interest in a career in opera because of his race. When he went to Memphis, it was slightly different; he shared:

> That was my initial exposure in that way to prejudice or to people shunning me because I was Black or whatever. But, I was lucky because the protection that I had in Memphis, because the program I was involved in was a university-sanctioned program that was supported by the state, so there had to be a certain amount of protection and a certain amount of support that they gave me whether I was Black or not. When George hired me, I played an audition for five different people on the staff. I found out later that the vote was unanimous that I should get that position. The whole question of race didn't come up then. As I got older though, it started dawning on me that I'm the only one.

In our interview, Maestro Waters defined himself as an African American. I asked him, "Why?" He responded, "I use them interchangeably." He went on to say, "There have been various movements even in my lifetime. People need that for identity. I don't need it in that way for identity." Gender and race impacted his college experiences, but mostly in terms of causing him to question his chosen profession:

> I don't know. Maybe deep down inside at some point I found myself asking, "Here I am a Black person. Is there any chance for me to be a concert pianist?" My teachers were very supportive. My piano teacher, Ivan Davis, accepted me as a piano student. I was the only undergraduate piano student he had ever had at the University of Miami. All the others were grad students, and he was still concertizing at that point, he wasn't around a lot, but he thought I was very talented so he decided to take me on. He had other Black students, so it was not a question of him needing to have a Black student.

He does not feel he needs to claim a racial identity in the way that some people do. When I asked him what influenced him to think this way, he shared this insight:

> Other people initially brought it up to me to say, you realize you are the only African American or the only Black, because at that time it was Black person doing what you are doing. Then I said, "Oh, you know you are right. That is the case." I am not saying that I was totally oblivious, but by the time I came back to the Greater Miami

Opera and the plan was for me to become Artistic Director, there was no question about... I mean this is not an equal opportunity. This is not an affirmative action type of thing. There are many, many other people out there who could have been chosen, who could have been hired for that position, but they chose me, and it wasn't because I was Black. It had to be because I had the chops to do the job. There would have been everything against them for them to hire me, but instead they took a chance, and it worked out very well.

His position on affirmative action is that it is necessary because people of color have been shut out for so long in many different ways. He said, "The doors were closed for so long, and some of the doors are still closed. There needs to be a boost. There needs to be someone who says, 'Okay, we are going to take a chance on this person and give them the opportunity.'" Yet, he does not think someone should be elevated to a position because of his or her race, but that a level of accomplishment and achievement should exist. He also does not feel affirmative action has been as successful as people think. He said, One could even argue that affirmative action has not been successful in many ways. Other than the entertainment and the athletic industry (maybe in some jobs like hospitals and such things) but where do you have an abundance of African Americans, Hispanics, or Asians in top positions? You don't. It doesn't exist. This position fascinated me because Maestro Waters' statement suggested a misunderstanding about the purpose of affirmative action. As I have argued before, (Cuyler, 2013), despite popular thought, the government did not design affirmative action to benefit unqualified people of color, women, or other protected classes. In fact, the government intended the policy to do exactly what it did in the Maestro's case, to identify and employ the most qualified person regardless of their race.

Maestro Waters and I discussed the belief that White women, more than any other protected class, have benefitted from affirmative action (Massie, 2016). Statistically, in 2006, more White women worked in opera management than people of color. He stated, "They have really gotten more and have been raised higher than any other group." He believed that his achievements and skills benefitted him more than affirmative action:

I don't think I was hired for any of these jobs because of affirmative action. I don't think I was hired for any of these jobs because I was Black. I think that the stakes were too high. You can't put somebody in a responsible position like at the San Francisco Opera or in Miami, being responsible for casting, being responsible for choosing repertoire and all that kind of stuff, just because they are Black,

Asian, or whatever. You have to have somebody who knows what he is doing, who knows what the audience wants. I personally don't think that affirmative action had anything to do with that.

I asked Maestro Waters if he had experienced what he believes to be racism or discrimination. He said, "Yes and no." He believes his achievements are well deserved because he worked hard. He attributed this philosophy of hard work to his racial background, relaying this insight:

I always felt, as most African Americans do, that you have to work harder. That is something that was ingrained in me not only from my parents and my family, but from other Black teachers who influenced me as I was getting towards the end of high school and college. Like at the University of Miami, one of the reasons I decided not to be a concert pianist is because I saw all those Cuban kids who were coming into the United States, and they had no problems staying in the practice room eight to ten hours a day and practicing. I just wasn't going to do that. I just did not feel excited about it enough, although when I was in high school I loved practicing piano, and I loved playing piano, and I still do love playing piano. But my focus just became different.

Yet, to a degree, he expressed that living as a person of color has hindered his participation in aspects of U.S. society. He shared this story:

I've rarely directly encountered racism. There have been a couple of instances that I could specifically point to, one of which was with an orchestra in the Midwest in which I was conducting a *Carmen* there. It was very obvious that this orchestra wasn't having it. I was walking down the hall, and there were about six members of the orchestra coming towards me. All six of them turned their heads and ignored me as I walked past them. I felt in rehearsal that there was a certain tension. I asked the string players to do a certain thing, part of this could be because I was a young conductor, and this was a big symphony orchestra. They just don't care about young conductors. It was hard for me to figure out at that moment. Of course, I wasn't thinking about it, I was just trying to get the job done, whether it was because I was Black or whether or not it was because I was a young conductor.

Maestro Waters also spoke about this incident in a 2001 issue of *Opera News* (Kellow, 2001). In our interview he stated, "Working with the

Memphis Symphony, in Jackson, Mississippi, Miami, and Arkansas, I never had any problems with the people. There might have been resistance, resentment, but they did what I asked them to do." He identified his experience in the Midwest as blatant and obvious resistance to his artistic leadership as a conductor; he expounded:

> It wasn't because I didn't know what I was doing. It was *Carmen*, which is the opera I have conducted more than any other. I know I knew it very well. One never knows because in this day and time people are just not going to say right out to you. But I have always been protected. When I went back to Miami, because I was being groomed to be Artistic Director, I got to know all the board members because they wanted me to attend all the meetings even before I became Artistic Director. Because of the position, people were obligated to invite me to private functions and country clubs. I mean I don't want to necessarily make it look as if they had to do it, but to a certain extent they did because there are certain social things that people have to do. If you're President or Chairman of the Board, and you have someone who is going to become Artistic Director, of course, you have to invite them to a party, and, of course, you have to invite them to private meetings and all those things. There are things that are inherent in the position. As General Director of this company, there are things that I am sure I get invited to, but people just feel it is something you have to do. Whether they like me or not, they have to do it.

Maestro Waters seemed very comfortable in bi-racial environments. Yet. he attended primarily Black American elementary, middle, and high schools. This puzzled me. I wanted to know more about how he developed the comfortability to relate to people of all walks of life racially. He credited his parents for bringing him up deeply religious. Also, two of his aunts worked for wealthy White people in Miami Beach. He visited and played with their kids often. These visits helped him to relate to others despite their racial backgrounds. One visit benefitted Maestro Waters in a very special way:

> There was a wealthy judge visiting from St. Louis. This lady, I will never forget her because we sang at her house before. She asked if we would come over and entertain. My middle name is Anthony, and they used to call me Tony. Then she said, "Tony, why don't you go ahead and play a couple of solo pieces?" I was studying piano at that time, so I did a couple of things. This judge was really

quite taken by it. He pulled my mother aside and said you know I think he is very talented. He paid for all my piano lessons until my freshman year in college. But that was one of the exposures that I had to White people. Going to the University of Miami, there were over 260 or so music majors, and there were eight Black music majors, and we obviously stuck together. That was my first exposure to the social part of dealing with that and just in dealing in general with people outside of my comfort zone.

He believes a person has to prepare for these kinds of situations. He said, "It became very obvious very quickly that we were looked at in a different way, in a positive way":

Any time anybody needed an accompanist, they came to me. We were also in the Chamber Singers. It was funny because of the 16 people in Chamber Singers, five of them were Black. Three of them were tenors, and I was one of them. We were all excellent musicians, we were all hard workers, and everybody knew it. Also we were aggressive, and we were ambitious. Anytime anybody wanted anything done, they would call on us to do it. To this day my professors, I'm still in touch with a lot of them, they relate back to those days when we were always the soloists, and we were always the number one, you know. We just realized because of our background and because of the teachers that we had in high school that you got to do not only well, you got to do better. That was a hell of a lot of pressure, especially back then because we are talking about the late 60s and early 70s. It was a constant thing where you had to watch your Ps and Qs all the time. We memorized all the music that we had to sing in university chorale. We became section leaders and all of that kind of stuff. We were not overly aggressive because you know you don't want to get to that point where people begin to dislike you, but it was very clear that we knew what we were doing and that we were accepted as such.

Maestro Waters maintains that he had a mission. He was determined to make it in the operatic world. He surrounded himself with the right people and placed himself in the right situations, but he said:

I don't know that a lot of it was really conscious. When the opera coach said, "You should come and work with me this summer on *Il Tabarro*," I didn't think twice about it. I am saying to myself, "This would give me a chance to work with this professional woman and to learn this piece, and I love opera." So why not? And when Mary Buckley said why not work with the opera workshop, when all these things, opportunities started presenting themselves, I am saying I have got to do it.

The transition from Memphis to San Francisco Opera was also challenging for Maestro Waters. As a 21 year old, he had no idea about what to expect. He said, "All I knew was that I was going to work for the second largest opera company in America in an administrative position." In Memphis, in his managerial experience he had dealt primarily with young singers and booking shows, but nothing on the level of his new position at San Francisco Opera. He shared:

> Mr. Adler wanted a conductor who was young enough and not itching to conduct but would be his personal musical assistant to help with casting, stage directors, and singers. I actually started looking at the San Francisco Opera because Leontyne sang there a lot. Everything revolved around Leontyne. There was a magazine, and I forget the name of the magazine, but Francis Ford Coppola, I think he owned the magazine. It just so happened in 1974, Leontyne opened the San Francisco Opera season in *Manon Lescaut*. Once I found out about this, I subscribed to the magazine because I figured there might be other things about Leontyne. I began, for some crazy reason, absorption of the whole San Francisco culture having no idea that within the next two years I was going to be living and working there. Just like a lot of the other things that happened in my life, it was sort of happenstance. Going to San Francisco and immediately realizing what this city was about, that this is a city that is about culture. It is a city that is about art. It is a city that is about fairness and openness and the San Francisco Opera. You know, my God, here I am in my first season, and it is going to be Sutherland, Pavarotti, Price, Söderström, Domingo; you know, all of these people and in a city that is so cultured.

He had to make a lot of adjustments because he was not entirely ready for all he would experience. He had some exposure to social behaviors in Miami working with the opera company, but because his position changed from rehearsal pianist and chorister to administrator, he realized he was perceived differently. He said, "It was a very, very shocking thing. I had to do a lot of learning very quickly." Social graces and etiquette regarding how to deal with people, responding to calls, and writing notes became more important. He said, "My parents did teach me, but you know when you are young like that you don't necessarily have to do it, and you are excused because of it, but now I am in a professional world. You have to carry yourself in a certain way."

Maestro Waters expressed that his racial identity as an African American became more important because all of a sudden he had a position of authority:

> I am in a position in which I have to tell people, "Yes, you can do this. No, you can't do that." I am a nice person and I hate to say, "No." But I have to understand that I got to say, "No." I have to keep relationships even though I do say, "No." Some people are not going to necessarily accept what I have to say, and some of that probably does come down to the racial thing, but again, there is enough respect for me, partially because I am the kind of person that I am, which is nice, but also because of my position. That is probably more than anything else, the position. It took a lot of adjusting very, very quickly.

The job required him to work 12 to 14 hours a day, six days a week, and often on Sundays. He held this position for four-and-a-half years. He said, "I was Mr. Adler's main assistant for artistic matters and later took on the responsibilities of Artistic Administrator, which meant negotiating contracts and all that. It was tough."

In terms of attracting African Americans to opera, Maestro Waters does not agree that people go to the theater to see someone like themselves on stage:

> On the other hand, last year, for example, when Angela Brown and Mark Rucker made their Met debuts, there was a noticeable bump in African Americans attending the Met. Now Black people go to the Met all the time because it is New York, but this was very different. Part of it was an orchestrated thing, because Angela was the first Black singer in a long time to make her debut there doing *Aïda*, and she had developed herself to a point where people were really watching her and watching her development and all. I mean, there were rows and rows and rows of Black people in the orchestra section. Now the Met ain't giving out no tickets. These people bought expensive tickets to see this sister sing *Aïda*. And the same thing with Mark Rucker.

In his work as an executive opera manager, he felt that he needed to establish and maintain a presence in the community. He has done a lot of work in schools with students. He thinks it is particularly important for students of color to see a potential role model:

> White kids get that, and they get those kinds of role models. Whether I like the term role model or the responsibility is a whole different thing. I think it is really important, and when I see kids, when they come up to me and they see who I am and what I do, they ask questions, and they want to know what it is like. I think it is very important, and I have got to serve that purpose. In Miami, the big question came up when I became Artistic Director, how much of that should we use? Do we not say that you are the first and only African American who is the Artistic Director of a major opera company? We wrestled with that for quite a while, and I decided that we should. They agreed because this is something that is news that is important for people to know. I like to think that eventually that's not necessary, but in this society and in this culture it's probably always necessary.

When I asked how he felt about diversity in executive opera management, he responded:

> There is no diversity. Now there are some in theater. There might be a couple in ballet, especially with Black dance companies, but those are not big companies. Symphony orchestras, I'm not in that world, so I don't really know.

At the time, OPERA America identified Maestro Waters as one of four executive opera managers of color serving at a major opera company in 2006 when I began collecting data for this study. He shared:

> It is the same thing about being an opera singer as opposed to being a rap star. You look at the money. You look at the fame and all of that, and you figure I could make more money and do much more and have a better life with this kind of stuff than going into opera. It is not something in the mainstream still. I have to say that we in this business haven't made it necessarily any more inviting for ethnic types to go into administration. You know, they look at it and see that there are so few people out there and think, "Why should I bother?" I certainly did not look at it as a trailblazing thing when Mr. Adler offered me the job in San Francisco. The reason I took it was because it was the San Francisco Opera, and Dr. Buckley had always said to me that I should learn what is happening backstage

to become an all-around person in the opera world. It was about the production aspect of opera and working with one of the leading opera impresarios and to find out how he casts and how an opera is put together at that level.

These opportunities served Maestro Waters well and helped him become the leader he is through trial, error, and experimentation. He learned management principles on the job because few Arts Management programs existed at that time. He shared:

> Mr. Adler liked things a certain way. This sort of goes back to something we talked about earlier in having to deal with the other aspects of the opera company, which was very interesting for me, looking at all the backstage stuff and working with the technical director and figuring out which productions can go together and can be in the house at the same time. If it's a new production with this director, how is that going to work versus a new production with another director? Who is going to direct this? What are the staffing requirements? I was responsible for all the assistant directors, the production assistants, the musical staff, everything. You have three or four operas either rehearsing or performing at the same time. We did not have computers in those days, so this was all done by hand.

Several Black opera singers influenced Maestro Waters' career development: Leontyne Price, but also Simon Estes and Martina Arroyo. He said, "Martina and Simon have probably been the biggest influences on my career in terms of helping me get to the next step."

It occurred to me that a force outside of himself served as motivation for pursuing a position at the executive level in opera management; he agreed:

> I thought I would do this for two years, and I would learn what happens backstage at the opera, especially at the San Francisco Opera, and I might meet Leontyne. Then I'll go back into conducting, which was what I wanted to do. I ended up staying there for four-and-a-half years. Then Martina called and said, "I am doing *Trovatore* in Detroit next fall." She wanted me to conduct it. She came to Memphis to do *Forza*. She had done *Aïda* in Miami in 1972, and I was in the chorus. I got to know her, and we kept in touch. So in Memphis two years later, there was this *Forza*, and I conducted the rehearsal without a score, and she was very impressed with that as were other people. She remembered that. When it came time for

the *Trovatore*, she said, "I am doing a production, and I'd like you to conduct it." I said I didn't know if I was going to leave the San Francisco Opera yet. She said, "Well, you have to decide at some point if you are going to remain an administrator or if you are going to be a conductor again." That was the catalyst that convinced me that now is the time.

In the spring of 1979, he resigned from his position at the San Francisco Opera and immediately received an invitation in Salt Lake City to conduct *Carmen*. That fall he received three more engagements. But, an old mentor from UM wanted him to return to Miami. Dr. Buckley wanted to groom him to become Artistic Director of the Greater Miami Opera. He served there for 14 years. At the end of his tenure in Miami, he hoped that someday he would become a General Director. The story of how he received the position he held at the Connecticut Opera at the time that we did his interview in 2006 is similar. He became Music Director and after three years the company decided to make a change. He shared this story:

They asked me if I would be General Director. That was a good possibility for me, but I said to them "I will not be the typical General Director. I don't deal with finances. I know how to read a balance sheet, but that is not my expertise. We will have to have someone else." They planned to hire a Managing Director to deal with the finances. I would deal with the board specifically, but the Managing Director would have that chief responsibility. I can deal with future planning; I can deal with community. I can deal with rebuilding the image of the company in the community and all of that. I will be the spokesperson for the company because I would be General Director. That is how this job happened.

We discussed the personal and professional qualities the board of directors used to select Maestro Waters as General/Artistic Director of Connecticut Opera:

I'm a nice person. I'm a fair person. I'm a passionate person. I passionately believe in what an opera company and what arts organizations in general have to do with the community, how they interact in the community. I'm a fair player. I'm a collaborator. Somebody on the board said, "When you speak, there is not only a clarity, but there is a passion that we get from you that brings us in, that you are a real spokesperson for the opera." That is because I love it. I mean there are people who say, this gets back to sort of a racial thing, but they say, "Well, you are so articulate, and you speak so well." Aren't I supposed to? I'm not the kind of person who is very confrontational about such things. Leontyne always says, "My protest is on the stage. Every time I go on the stage and do a good performance, that's breaking down another door." I really think that is where it is. I never got out and marched, I came up during the Civil Rights era. I figured the more I do well, the better it is for not only me but for everybody else in the community.

In the application and interview process for the position he held at the time we conducted his interview, he did not experience any challenges; he said, "I tell you; I have been lucky. The only one was from the University of Miami to Memphis State, and that was the audition I had." A formal and informal network helped to advance his career. He told this story about his interview and audition for San Francisco Opera:

> We would always list the roles that singers sang. At the time, Mr. Adler was casting *Flying Dutchman*, and it didn't have a Senta. We are sitting there; Richard Rezinski was my predecessor, they would go over the names and everything. He gave me two sets of cards. One was the artist and the other was the role, so Senta and all the people who sung the role. He told me to look at the card, and he said, "Who are some of the people who are not listed on that card?" I came up with two names, one of which was Gwyneth Jones. He called Richard and said that Gwyneth was not on this card. They both looked at each other, and they were really shocked. That was one of the things that clinched it because he said later, "You have the most encyclopedic knowledge of opera and opera singers of any young person that I have ever met." I lived, ate, slept, drank opera and still do.

When I asked him about the realities of being an executive opera manager, he spoke about the difficulties caused by the arts landscape changing. At the Greater Miami Opera there was an abundance of funding and high-quality performances. But, a transition in finances and artistic standards caused opera companies to stop engaging famous opera stars. He thinks people attending opera to have an operatic experience also caused a problem. Not to mention the competitive, for-profit entertainment sector. The nature of the job functions of an executive opera manager might also detour people's interest in the career path, he added:

> It does not seem to be a worthy investment until the economy changes around or people's ideas and practices in terms of

supporting arts organizations gets better. On the other hand, young singers are flocking to opera more than they ever have. Our opera guild does a competition in April, and we had 170 applicants, and it was a very small competition. When we go to New York for auditions, we have sometimes 600 to 700 people request auditions. That is typical, not only for the opera companies, but for the competitions and the young artist programs. They are out there, and they want to do this. I think that is very encouraging. But, you just have to say, how many jobs are there?

Because of my background as someone who studied voice with the intentions of becoming an opera singer, I wondered how many of these singers, particularly those of color, might serve opera better by becoming opera managers. However, Maestro Waters pointed this out:

> Well, who knows? It is hard to say because we are not often that visible unless you are the General or Artistic Director. I thought at one point, actually, more than one point, that it was important for me to continue doing this for exactly that reason, because we want to get more African Americans and more Hispanics in the top level of opera management. I say to as many people that give any indication they were interested that they should go and do something about it. Again, it is a question of whether or not you think it is an investment.

When I asked Maestro Waters what changes he would make in the course of his career path, if any, he said that it would probably not be the same:

> I probably would have taken some business courses because it would have put me in a slightly different situation. Everything I know I learned from having been there. I got to know a lot of General Directors of opera companies, not only Mr. Adler, but Carol Fox at the Lyric Opera of Chicago and Mark Feinstein of Washington.

He expressed that he might have chosen a slightly different career path with more conducting, as opposed to management and conducting:

> I applied and was accepted and got to the finals of the Exxon conducting program. The finals were with the Indianapolis Symphony on the morning I would have a dress rehearsal of *Macbeth* here. That would have been a career choice and investment, but I had no

idea of the results, so I stayed here instead. You can't make it as a conductor just doing opera in this country. In Europe you can, but in this country you can't. In terms of a career trajectory, I probably would have gone the route of symphonic to get that experience. I had an operatic background I could have transferred. I think that has hampered me in terms of my career because I don't get the engagements. I did quite a bit of orchestral conducting in Europe. I have done some of it here, but my focus here was opera. I think my career path would have gotten bigger and better had I chosen that other route. I don't regret what I have done, but in retrospect I think things would have gone quite differently had I done that.

Yet, he does not think his career path is different from White executive opera managers.

At the time of our interview, Maestro Waters did not have mentees, but he shared this advice for executive opera manager aspirants:

You need to be involved with an opera company backstage where you can see the workings of the opera company backstage. One needs to have access to the managers to be able to see daily what goes on in terms of running the company and how the various components work together, how it works with not just the artistic administration, but production staff, development, marketing/PR. You have to be able to immerse yourself in the inner workings of the opera company. An effective General Director needs to also know what the chorus is doing, what the costume situation is like, how long it takes to load in a set. Is the set going to be too big or too small and all those things. It is not a part of coursework. It is a part of being there and being around. That is the only way to do it. You have just got to be there and really see and really talk to people and to see it in action. As much as I love and appreciate classrooms, they take you only so far. Then you just have to be out there in the field doing it.

He is not sure that ten years from now he still wants to serve as General or Artistic Director of a major opera company. Conducting is his passion. He said, "It is what I think I do better than anything else." He likes his work enough that he would ideally like to become the General Director of an opera company at a higher level. He shared this ambition:

I don't know that it is in the cards that I would run a company at level one because it is just too complicated, but the next level of companies, Seattle and San Diego, and places we in the business agree are generally well run. Those are places that one could use as a model. I would like to become General Director of a company like Atlanta, or I have in the back of my mind Michigan Opera Theatre. I have this idea in my mind that I want to be the General Director of a company in an area that has a lot of Black people because I want to get more Black people involved in opera, not just Black people but more ethnic people. That is one of the reasons I stick with Houston Ebony Opera.

In addition to his position as the General/Artistic Director of Connecticut Opera, Maestro Waters served as the Artistic Director for the Houston Ebony Opera Guild. This African American opera company hosted summer residencies for young artists and presented summer opera. Examining the dichotomy that exists between African, LatinX, Asian, Arab, and Indigenous (ALAAI) opera companies and legacy opera companies can become problematic career-wise for students of color. Both organizations need highly effective managers of color; however, ALAAI opera companies, historically, have lacked the financial stability and infrastructure on which one could build a successful career. He added this insight:

> I think it is a false hope for any of us to think that we are going to develop an African American opera company in this day and age in a way that we would be proud of it, in a way that it would really make an impact, a difference. It's unfortunate, because opera is still isolated to a certain extent and is not in the mainstream as much as we would like it to be. Although opera is popular enough, but it is not popular in the Black community. You know, it is not a community in which it has been important enough.

He thinks that gender and race should not factor into succeeding as an executive opera manager, saying, "But, that's ideal. I don't know that it has been tested enough because there just have not been enough of us. There has been Linda, there has been me, and just a couple of other people. You don't have enough people there to even say." Yet, the barriers he thinks people face are individual because it is a question of whether someone wants to create a career in opera management realizing U.S. society's perceptions of the arts in communities and the lack of financial support for the arts. He stated, "Somebody said to me once, 'Why would anybody want to jump on a sinking ship?'" He does not believe opera, and the arts in general, are a sinking ship, but he said:

You look at the big corporations laying off 10, 15, 30,000 people. The people that have these million-dollar corporations. It just does not look good anywhere, so why would anybody want to go into the nonprofit arts, which by its nature is going to be less financially rewarding because in this day and time the finances make a huge difference. We went into it because we loved opera. You know we could sustain ourselves, but now because things are so expensive and because people want so much and there is so much out there, you have to make a living. It is hard to do.

Still, he is adamant that people of color should pursue careers in opera management only if they love it:

You have got to love it, and that is the way it is with any art form. In the 1970s, there were about 30 professional opera companies in America. Now there are about 125 to 130 something.

In reading Joe Volpe's book, it reminded me that what Maestro Waters says is absolutely true. The Met stopped touring because regional opera companies began to spring up all over the place. In the cities where the Met used to tour, local companies exists. Even though the Met suggests a certain quality of production, regional opera companies challenged the managerial rationale for the Met tours. It also occurred to me that the Metropolitan Opera's discontinuation of regional tours caused an uprising of home-grown companies that challenged communities to support them and to make investments in the cultural life of their communities. In Hartford, Maestro Waters experienced an interesting phenomenon. Residents would not attend Connecticut Opera performances because of their support for the Metropolitan Opera. During his time at Connecticut Opera, he worked to change this practice by raising the standard of the artistic product. He said, "The only way to solidify your face and to get people to come and keep them coming is to have a good artistic product. Everything else is ancillary."

I consider Maestro Waters a risk-taker because of his career path. As stated earlier, he is one of four African Americans to have served as an executive-level opera manager at a major opera company in the U.S. Yet, he does not consider himself a risk-taker when it comes to his work in opera management:

I really am basically traditional and conservative. That is the way I was raised. All the artistic environments that I have been in have been that way, and that is how I am. My charge here was to turn the company around in terms of improving the artistic product and improving the relations with the city and with the artistic community so that we were looked at as a serious organization. We successfully did that. In the meantime, you can't take risks. Then the economy collapses, and people stop going to the opera for whatever reason. You take surveys and realize people are saying, "We love *Bohème.* We love *Aïda.* We love *Carmen.* That is what we are going to support." I argue with Linda and others about this all the time. I mean, somebody who has never been to an opera as far as I can see is not going to necessarily be enticed to go and see *Nixon in China* more than they would be enticed to go and see *La Bohème, Madame Butterfly,* or *Aïda.* That is one of our big problems, of course, even with people who are regular opera lovers. Getting them to the opera house to see something unusual is the hard part.

I consider him a trailblazer in his career. He did not agree entirely. He believes the trailblazing he has done is because he stayed the course. He expounded upon this by sharing:

There was a conscious effort to stick with this administrative thing once I started doing it, but to be able to conduct along the way. Yes, I think that if there is any trailblazing it is because I am still one of few African Americans. I guess just by the nature of that situation, you could say that I am a trailblazer. I've been so concerned with keeping my reputation so that people trust and believe me and take me seriously not only as an arts administrator, but there is just a certain level of accomplishment of achievement that you have to have, and it has to be consistent. You know that statement, "It is less important to get a job than to get the second job." You know, it is more difficult to remain a success than to be a success. If they realize that the work I am doing is good, then that makes it easier and better for the next person.

Although he does not consider himself a risk-taker or trailblazer, he is cognizant of the fact that he did something that few people of his race, only four, has done:

A lot of the Black singers in New York look at me as a hope for them. A few of them have said this, "You should bring all these Black singers to Connecticut, and you could cast an all-Black *Don Giovanni.* I could cast an all-Black anything, but I am not going to do it because that to me is not what I am here for."

I find it fascinating that Maestro Waters considered the impact his career would have on opera managers of color of the future. Ensuring a career legacy creates opportunities for others is not always easy. When I considered his interview in the sum of the five other respondents in this book, all of them are cognizant of keeping the career path open for opera managers of color of the future. Maestro Waters currently serves as Assistant Professor of Music at SUNY Binghamton University.

References

Cuyler, A. C. (2013). Affirmative action and diversity: Implication for arts management. *Journal of Arts Management, Law, and Society*, 43(2), 98–105.

Kellow, B. (2001). One the beat. *Opera News*, 66(5), 10.

Massie, V. (2016). *White women benefit most from affirmative action – and are among its fiercest opponents*. Accessed December 13, 2019. www.vox.com/2016/5/25/11682950/fisher-supreme-court-white-women-affirmative-action.

Okahana, H., & Zhou, E. (2019). *Graduate enrollment and degrees: 2008 to 2018*. Accessed December 13, 2019. https://cgsnet.org/ckfinder/userfiles/files/CGS_GED18_Report_web.pdf.

8 The Finale: Conclusions

Introduction

This book aimed to: (1) explore the impact of race on the careers of executive opera managers of color in the U.S., (2) identify beneficial experiences to their careers, (3) describe factors that advanced or served as barriers to their careers, (4) identify career strategies, (5) contemplate how opera might attract and retain more racially diverse managers, and lastly (6) serve as inspiration for Arts Management professionals and students around the globe who may view their class, different ability, ethnicity, gender, race, or sexual orientation as a liability in their pursuit of executive-level management careers in Arts Management.

Chapters 2–7 revealed that executive opera managers of color in the U.S. entered opera management through a variety of artistic entry points. These entry points included composer, conductor, director, manager, singer, and stage manager. Though Wayne Brown sang in college, his primary entry point into executive opera management came by way of management through his previous roles with orchestras and the National Endowment for the Arts (NEA). None of the executive opera managers of color viewed their career as different from their White colleagues. Yet, none of the respondents has held an executive-level position at an OPERA America level 1 opera company whose budget size is $15 million or above.

Given the variety of entry points into executive opera management, readers should also note that none of the executives of color in this book earned a degree in Arts Administration or Arts Management. In fact, Wayne Brown, Linda Jackson, and Wille Anthony Waters stated that Arts Administration or Arts Management degree programs did not exist during the time that they pursued their higher education. However, this statement is inaccurate. Arts Administration educators established the earliest formal courses in Arts Administration in 1966, following the first

National Council on the Arts' suggestion in 1964–1965 (National Endowment for the Arts, 1965, p. 18). With the proliferation of Arts Management degree programs, one could argue that students of color who study Arts Management today and want to pursue careers in opera management are better positioned to do so than the executives of color profiled in this book. Alas, times have changed. In addition to people living and working longer, the access to opportunities for aspiring opera managers of color has been delayed.

Because only one woman of color and no LatinX, Arab, or Indigenous People have managed opera companies at the executive level, it appears that arts managers among these marginalized and oppressed gender and racial identities may experience more difficulty pursuing and attaining careers in executive opera management. The opera industry should ask itself, why? Furthermore, based on Michael Ching's comment below, and the success of my White, cisgender male, gay identified former students, one could reason that identifying as White, cisgender male, and gay aids one's pursuit of a career in executive opera management in the U.S.

> All three of the finalists for this job had wives. Statistically, this field is not run by heterosexuals, so there was something going on that maybe was never written down on a piece of paper. So some things work for you and some things work against you. Statistically, if there are three finalists for a job as an Artistic Director you would think you would have at least one gay person.

In the subsequent sections of this chapter, I will describe the experiences that executive opera managers of color in the U.S. viewed as beneficial to their careers. I will also describe the factors that they believed advanced or served as barriers to their careers and could impact potential opera managers of color. In addition, I will suggest the strategies that executive opera managers of color in the U.S. used to successfully manage their careers in opera. Lastly, as the service arts organization for opera in the U.S. and arguably the leader of the opera industry, I will critically examine OPERA America's current ADEI efforts and offer suggestions that I believe will advance and enhance the seismic institutionalization of racial ADEI in opera companies, if led effectively by OPERA America.

Beneficial experiences

Across the six career narratives in Chapters 2–7, three beneficial career experiences emerged as essential for setting opera managers of color in the U.S. on their paths to executive-level positions: early exposure to arts education, pre-collegiate extracurricular arts activities, and their artistic careers before attaining managerial positions. Table 8.1 displays the beneficial experience articulated and the executive opera manager of color who identified the said experience in their career narrative.

Exposure to arts education

Of these three key beneficial experiences identified, the quotes below from the respondents support the significance of early exposure and pre-collegiate extracurricular arts activities. For example, when speaking about the importance of early exposure to arts education, Mr. Akina stated, "the excitement of the theater was something, that really inspired me at that time." Mr. Ching shared that he began studying piano at age six.

Torrie Allen: As a kid, I have a very strong memory with my mom, watching a TV show called *Gomer Pyle* and hearing the actor playing Gomer, Jim Nabors, sing "The Impossible Dream." And, on one episode of the *Dinah Shore Show*, Robert Goulet sang "If Ever I Would Leave You." As a kid, I remember locking into the deep, dark, and bright timbre of those two voices and wanting to have that kind of a sound.

Table 8.1 Beneficial experiences

Beneficial experience	Executive opera manager
Artistic career	H. Akina T. Allen W. Brown M. Ching L. Jackson W. Waters
Early exposure to arts education	H. Akina T. Allen W. Brown M. Ching L. Jackson W. Waters
Pre-collegiate extracurricular arts activities	H. Akina T. Allen W. Brown M. Ching L. Jackson W. Waters

Wayne Brown: Miss Martin was my music teacher in the fourth grade. This was in the public schools of Detroit, Winterhalter School. I remember my first violin classes in elementary school. Another early influence in elementary school was my art teacher where we had the opportunity of working with sculpture. The third component was an involvement with the stage crew.

Linda Jackson: I'm not sure why, but I ended up with a group of friends who put the shows on in high school. I think that contributed a lot to sort of how I got involved in this.

Willie Anthony Waters: My earliest memory of opera is when my sister sang the "Inflammatus" from Rossini's *Stabat Mater*. Our high school chorus presented it, and she was the soprano soloist. I was knocked away because of the high C's at the end. Then her last year at FAMU we all drove up for her graduation. The chorus did the "Halleluiah" from King of Kings with band.

Career advancers

Through my discussions with the respondents, five factors emerged that they believed helped to advance their careers into executive opera management: family, mentors, network (formal and informal), self, and serendipity. In Table 8.2, I show the factor and the respondent whose career narrative supports the factor. The quotes below support the believability and credibility of the factors as supported by the specific respondents.

Family

Linda Jackson: No one ever said, "You shouldn't be doing that. There is no money in opera. Why don't you be a doctor?"

Willie Anthony Waters: They all came in mass for the first couple of years. My oldest sister, of course, was very interested. My mother would always go and drag a couple of my aunts along with her. My two younger sisters, initially, would go because it was an exciting thing for them to see their brother up there conducting an opera. My oldest sister and brother knew more about it than the others did, so they would go even when some of the others wouldn't. Initially, they all went and dragged my little nieces and nephews along. One of my nieces went to a couple of operas last year. She said, "It was because of the experience I had when you were there conducting, so I really got to like it."

Mentorship

Linda Jackson: David is very much devoted to the art form and to exploring and pushing its boundaries. Bob was much more regimented

Table 8.2 Career advancers

Career advancers	Executive opera manager
Family	H. Akina T. Allen M. Ching L. Jackson W. Waters
Mentors	H. Akina T. Allen W. Brown M. Ching L. Jackson W. Waters
Network (formal and informal)	H. Akina T. Allen W. Brown M. Ching L. Jackson W. Waters
Self	H. Akina T. Allen W. Brown M. Ching L. Jackson W. Waters
Serendipity	H. Akina T. Allen W. Brown M. Ching L. Jackson W. Waters

and taught me a lot about discipline. From Cynthia I learned that you cannot have an opera unless you have competent people who get along and function as a group together. Interpersonal relationships within the staff are tantamount to having a successful company. Jane was also just very daring in terms of the way she just sort of put Texas Opera Theater together. We used to argue a lot, and that taught me a lot, too, because it helped me identify the things that I knew I did not want to do.

Willie Anthony Waters: Martina called and said, "I am doing *Trovatore* in Detroit next fall." She wanted me to conduct it. She had done *Aïda* in Miami in 1972, and I was in the chorus. I got to know her. So in Memphis two years later, there was this *Forza*, and I conducted the rehearsal without a score, and she was very impressed with that as were other people. She remembered that. When it came time for the *Trovatore*, she said, "I am doing a production, and I'd like you to conduct it." I said I didn't know if I was going to leave the San Francisco Opera yet. She said, "Well, you have to decide at some point if you are going to remain an administrator or if you are going to be a conductor again." That was the catalyst that convinced me that now is the time.

Network

Linda Jackson: Going from Chautauqua to BAM, even that, Mickey wanted to bring Opera Ebony to Brooklyn. She asked if there were any Black opera administrators out there; she did not know anything about opera. She called me and said she needed an opera administrator there.

Willie Anthony Waters: Leontyne Price, but also Simon Estes and Martina Arroyo. Martina and Simon have probably been the biggest influences on my career in terms of helping me get to the next step.

Self

Torrie Allen: The day that I auditioned for the Met Guild, I was downstairs at the Metropolitan Opera. I was singing one of Figaro's arias from the *Marriage of Figaro*. While I was singing, I had a weird out-of-body experience. I was thinking to myself, "I'm not in character right now. I'm just singing a song. I don't know if I want to do this." Plácido Domingo and Denise Graves were directly above me rehearsing *Samson and Delilah*, and I was saying to myself, "I just wanted to know I could do this, get to this level. I just wanted to know I had the chops to get to this level. I don't want this life anymore. I want more from the arts."

Wayne Brown: Well, I knew that I wanted to do something meaningful in the arts, but I was not always sure what that would be. I wouldn't necessarily say it impeded. Perhaps there were steps that I was introduced to various options along the way, which might have otherwise enabled me to have make a decision sooner than later. But I think ultimately, it all helped to better inform a better appreciation for what I do now. So I don't necessarily see any distractions along the way. I don't necessarily think of them as derailing, but indeed helping to enrich, enliven the curiosity and the interest, the passion for what I do.

Willie Anthony Waters: In terms of a career trajectory, I probably would have gone the route of symphonic to get that experience. I had an operatic background I could have transferred. I think that has hampered me in terms of my career because I don't get the engagements.

Serendipity

Linda Jackson: I was in the Assistant Managing Director position, which put me in charge of everything when Cynthia (Auerbach) found out she had lung cancer. She died two months before the season started. At that point, everything was in play, so we just let the season run, and at the end of the season they said, "Well, you know what you are doing." I didn't have any choice. I was production manager in Houston, and I was sort of Managing Director at Chautauqua, and Cynthia died. Then they asked me to be General Director. Then suddenly I was a General Director.

Willie Anthony Waters: Out of the clear blue sky I walked into the University of Miami School of Music and looked on the bulletin board, and there is an announcement from Memphis State University for a new program in operatic coaching and conducting, which would be run by George Osborne. The person in charge of the actual participants would be Kip Cutchstedder, Mignon Dunn's husband. I applied, the next week George called and asked if I would come to Memphis for an interview and audition. They flew me to Memphis, and I went, auditioned, and he offered me the job on the spot. It was a new program, half-sponsored by the state, half-sponsored by the university. I didn't have to put any money into it. It was a complete free ride.

Career barriers

The respondents discussed a range of perceived career barriers that they faced, or that potential opera managers of color could face in their pursuit of a career in opera management. These included that opera management is a hidden career, job duties, lack of competitive salary, lack of diversity, lack of interest in opera, and self. Though not all of the respondents' narratives support all of the factors, I use quotes below for a few of the career barriers to support my observation that these factors are indeed career barriers.

Opera, competitive salary, diversity, hidden career, and job duties

Linda Jackson: More than just opera being a European art form is working against it. There is no money. It is expensive. It is not for profit. It is hard to make a living. Given the kind of work I do here, if I worked for a corporation I would make three times as much money, but I don't think there are barriers necessarily in terms of administration. I just think it is not a choice that people are going to make. There are not White people making the choice at this point, either. There is going to be a void soon if we don't address how to deal with it. It is about compensation packages, and some of it is about just the workload and support systems that there are for nonprofit.

Willie Anthony Waters: I have to say that we in this business haven't made it necessarily any more inviting for ethnic types to go into administration. You know, they look at it and see that there are so few people out there and think, "Why should I bother?"

Self

> Michael Ching: My barriers are self-imposed. I admit that I would be farther along, if I wanted.
>
> Willie Anthony Waters: I think my career path would have gotten bigger and better had I chosen that other route. I don't regret what I have done, but in retrospect I think things would have gone quite differently had I done that.

Although most of the respondents do not feel that they experienced racism and sexism in their pursuit of executive positions in opera, in their interviews they shared stories that might interest aspiring opera managers of color, or those who are otherwise discriminated against, marginalized, or oppressed while pursuing professional careers in societies. As the only woman of color to achieve such a position in opera, Linda Jackson's perspective is truly unique and speaks volumes about intersectionality and the complex challenge of managing two or more marginalized and oppressed social identities while trying to manage a career or simply live. Indeed, individuals have identities that intersect and parallel in ways that impact how societies view, treat, and understand them, as well as how they understand themselves and the opportunities they see as available for themselves and their lives (Crenshaw, 1989).

Racism

> Torrie Allen: Beyond overt instances of racism, from my perspective, the real problem was the overwhelming amount of constant micro-aggressions. The sad thing is that a lot of good folk really didn't see themselves and their actions as aggressive. It was a horrible state of affairs that hurt performers of color and diminished the potential vibrancy of the entire industry. It was painful to hear stories about how the accumulation of this stuff made some people have nervous breakdowns because of having to wear White makeup or having to negotiate sexual harassment. I had to wear White makeup. They'd say, oh, if you want to sing this role, you're going to have to wear White makeup. Ugly, brutal, and it was really happening as recently as the 1990s!
>
> I was leading Anchorage Opera. We were in New York City auditioning singers, our Musical Director's there, I'm there. I sensed that a lot of the agents and singers were surprised to see me (a person of color) behind the table. I mean, I don't think that they knew that I had just as much or more real-life training and professional performance experience than them. This well-known agent came in and he's looking at my Musical Director. Right there in front of me, he's saying to him, "Watch out for these people." I was like, "What?" It was so shocking that I didn't act then. As I reflect on

it now. I should've just asked him to leave. It was so unbelievably disrespectful, racist, and all that is bad about the legacy mindset.

Michael Ching: Everyone assumes if you are Black, you are from here, unless you speak like you're from the Caribbean, or some African country. They assume your family has roots here, but I can go somewhere and someone will think I just got off some boat. It annoys me because my family has been here for a long time.

Linda Jackson: It is more about, you know, going to a cast party with a group of people who may or may not be prejudiced. It is not about, "Oh she's Black; she should not be stage managing." It is "Oh is it going to be okay to be at this person's home or something like that." You know, at first when I started in Houston, which was for better or worse, the South, and the same thing is true of Florida. You are a little bit conscious of that, but as time goes on and people get to know you and accept you, it goes away.

During my years on the board of OPERA America, we would have a lot of discussions about diversity at opera companies. Well, we have a hard time finding good singers of color who have been trained, particularly Blacks. I think that the ability to financially afford what you need to do is very difficult on young African Americans. It's hard on White singers, too. They would say, "What are we going to do?" I would say things like, "You know, you don't have to just hire Black singers. You can hire a Black receptionist. You don't have to like opera to be a receptionist. You don't have to like opera to be a finance director. It's a job."

Willie Anthony Waters: There have been a couple of instances that I could specifically point to, one of which was with an orchestra in the Midwest in which I was conducting a *Carmen* there. It was very obvious that this orchestra wasn't having it. I was walking down the hall, and there were about six members of the orchestra coming towards me. All six of them turned their heads and ignored me as I walked past them. I felt in rehearsal that there was a certain tension. I asked the string players to do a certain thing, part of this could be because I was a young conductor, and this was a big symphony orchestra. They just don't care about young conductors. It was hard for me to figure out at that moment. Of course, I wasn't thinking about it, I was just trying to get the job done, whether it was because I was Black or whether or not it was because I was a young conductor.

I mean there are people who say, this gets back to sort of a racial thing, but they say, "Well, you are so articulate, and you speak so well." Aren't I supposed to?

Sexism

Linda Jackson: There are times when I bring it on myself. I know my voice pitches up when I am angry or excited or trying to make a point, and I wish it didn't. I would probably be better at that if I was a male, but I do think that there are times when I realize it would have been a lot easier to make the case if I was a guy in a business suit in a room with a bunch of businessmen.

The female thing I don't think has kept me from participating in things. I think that we are in a time where that would be politically incorrect. It is just a question of how much harder you have to work to make an impact.

Career strategies

Relative to career strategies, when I asked respondents what advice they would give to aspiring opera managers of color, they suggested six career strategies: experience, knowledge, passion, perseverance, self, and work ethic. I included quotes that speak to the essence of the advice given by individual respondents. In Table 8.3, I also present the strategy and identify the respondent whose advice supports the strategy.

Advice

Henry Akina: I think that if you can study, you should with a program because they have productions and you're interested in productions. I would expect that you would learn the basics of playing instruments and reading music. I suppose that anyone who came to me would know that to begin with. I think that's an important part of it, but I don't think that's all of it.

Wayne Brown: I would encourage anyone who's interested to learn as much as you can about the art form. That comes about through reading; it comes about through experiencing. Whether that's performance or other arts settings. Networking is critical. Being patient, and yet tenacious, and taking full advantage of every step along the way. To absorb and schedule informational interviews. Quite often people think in terms of interviews have to be job related, but interviews can be invaluable in terms of obtaining insight from those to whom you'd like to be better informed about the nature of their work. There are areas outside of the art world that can be equally informative. How to manage a business. Working on your interpersonal skills, making sure there's effective communication. Managing projects. Immersing yourself in various cultures and languages. I would say those who have, perhaps a strong interest in the law, there are roles that can be played for someone who has a law degree. Increasingly, if we think about licensing and union contracts, those are all areas that can be of benefit to someone who's involved in Arts Management or in the role of leadership with an opera company.

Linda Jackson: You just keep doing it. I figure sooner or later they are going to get it or not. You can spend a lot more time trying to explain things and justify things. It really does just sort of force you to look at things differently, but when you are dealing with people who aren't

Table 8.3 Career strategies

Career strategies	Executive opera manager
Experience	H. Akina T. Allen W. Brown M. Ching L. Jackson W. Waters
Knowledge	H. Akina T. Allen W. Brown M. Ching L. Jackson W. Waters
Passion	H. Akina T. Allen W. Brown M. Ching L. Jackson W. Waters
Perseverance	H. Akina T. Allen W. Brown M. Ching L. Jackson W. Waters
Self	H. Akina T. Allen W. Brown M. Ching L. Jackson W. Waters
Work ethic	H. Akina T. Allen W. Brown M. Ching L. Jackson W. Waters

listening the first time, you find different ways to look at everything, and in the process you refine and make the arguments better for yourself.

If you can be at a company where it is really hands-on, you can really understand how the shows go together, and it will also help you figure out whether or not you can deal with people. If you can deal with artists and artists' egos and all of that, then you have a better shot at being a good administrator long term, whether it is opera or any place for that matter. The rest of it just sort of depends on your intuition and your instincts. Part of it overall is just dealing with people.

Willie Anthony Waters: You need to be involved with an opera company backstage where you can see the workings of the opera company backstage. One needs to have access to the managers to be able to see daily what goes on in terms of running the company and how the various components work together, how it works with not just the artistic administration, but production staff, development, marketing/PR. You have to be able to immerse yourself in the inner workings of the opera company. An effective General Director needs to also know what the chorus is doing, what the costume situation is like, how long it takes to load in a set. Is the set going to be too big or too small and all those things. It is not a part of coursework. It is a part of being there. You have just got to be there and really see and really talk to people and to see it in action.

Mentorship

The interviews revealed further insights that warrant further attention related to mentorship, racial identity development, and specific, measurable, achievable, relevant, and time-bound (SMART) approaches to successfully managing ADEI. Torrie Allen is the only respondent actively mentoring the next generation of arts managers. Michael Ching's quote below reveals the essence at the heart of the disparate behaviors around mentorship, while Torrie Allen's response provides insight into the role that good mentorship can play in advancing careers.

> Michael Ching: We tend to view helping someone else as not being in your best interest, but once you are in this field helping people is in your best interest.
>
> Torrie Allen: Yes, my staff and other young folk I intersect with. I've had good leaders and not-so-good leaders. I try my best to improve on the modeling from the very best leaders, because the not-so-good leaders really can have a toxic impact on your psyche. I often ask my staff if they feel like I'm empowering them enough. Above and beyond this, I champion efforts to open doors for new voices and ideas.

If all of the executive opera managers of color in the U.S. benefitted from mentorship and identified it as a key career advancer, and only one of them actively mentors aspiring opera or arts managers of color, this partially explains why there are fewer executive opera managers of color today than in 2007 when I first began collecting data for this book. In addition, during our interviews, Torrie Allen and Wayne Brown made the case for the importance of cross-cultural mentorship. In fact, Torrie reminded me of the quote, "Not all skinfolk are kinfolk" attributed to Zora Neale Hurston. In sum, the quote means that just because a person in a position of power may identify as Asian, Black, or as any other marginalized or oppressed identity, it does not mean that they will aid, help, mentor, or support another person with the same marginalized or oppressed identity. In my view, internalized racism causes this undermining and competitive behavior (Bivens, 2005).

Racial identity development

Racial identity development emerged as a theme of interest in this book. The respondents shared insights about how they personally managed or responded to issues relative to race in their personal and professional lives. For example, Michael Ching credited the Asian cultural values of hard work, discipline, and study as important to his development. He and other respondents shared the following:

Michael Ching: I think it made me a little bit obsessed with having a regular paycheck, and so except for maybe two or three months of an essentially 25-year career, I have never not had a regular paycheck.

In our household, you'd have to look hard to figure out an Asian lives there; there are a few things, even here in my office. Feng Shui, I'm usually facing the door. There is an Asian-looking teapot over there. I do drink tea. There is green tea in there. See, it is just one of those things that for me it actually hasn't been an issue.

Linda Jackson: I am honestly glad I did not grow up White. It is not because I was a big Black pro-whatever. It is just that I don't think I would have the sensitivity that I have if I had been raised as something comfortable. I mean I think the challenges that have been presented to me because I am a woman and because I am Black have made me a better person. I am not sure I would have had those same challenges if I had just been raised a White male, upper middle class, or something else. I am not sure I would have the same humility.

Becoming the first and only Black woman to run an opera company is important for that reason, which is stupid, as opposed to it just being important because I'm capable of running an opera company.

Willie Anthony Waters: I always felt, as most African Americans do, that you have to work harder. That is something that was ingrained in me not only from my parents and my family, but from other Black teachers who influenced me as I was getting towards the end of high school and college.

SMART approaches to successfully managing ADEI

Nonprofits use a variety of approaches to manage ADEI (Marrow, 2018). In our interview, Wayne Brown advocated for a holistic approach, and shared that he thought focusing on executive opera managers of color alone was too narrow. In retrospect, as shown in the quote below, I wonder why Mr. Brown values the Sphinx Organization's focus on placing African American and LatinX orchestral musicians differently than a program that might focus on placing executive opera managers of color at major opera companies? A program with a laser focus on executive opera managers might similarly yield a 4% increase in 11 years. Opera would benefit greatly from said change given that, currently, only one executive opera manager in the U.S., Mr. Brown, identified as a person of color.

Wayne Brown: I remember the early part of my career with the Detroit Symphony, my charge was to create a tally of every orchestra. I remember reaching out, how many in Minnesota, Baltimore, Brooklyn, etc. The Sphinx Organization has particular resonance for me because it was the first time a formalized effort was made to, it's not about head count, what kind of structure could be put in place to encourage putting more people in the pipeline. It resulted in a 1.5% membership of symphony orchestras that were occupied by African Americans specifically, not just the issue of diversity, but African American, to as much as 3–4% following 11 years of operation with the Sphinx Organization. It may not seem a lot, the scale of orchestras in the U.S. is large, but it's been profound. Even within the last year, the steps that the League has taken in terms of its publications, it's being thoughtful, mindful of optics, making sure that at any given convening, what does the table look like? What does the room look like? Are we creating engaging moments for participants? OPERA America is beginning to do something of a similar nature.

OPERA America's ADEI initiatives

On its website, OPERA America expressed that it believes that opera companies have an obligation to reflect their communities and that the art form and the industry gain from diversity, equity, and inclusion (OPERA America, 2020). The service arts organization provided the following definitions of diversity, equity, and inclusion specific to opera for its members:

• **Diversity:** Different perspectives, cultural histories, life experiences, and personal stories enrich the style, scale, and subject of new works and the interpretations of the inherited repertoire, as well as stimulate innovation at the organizational level. Diversity and gender parity recognize the richness of our varied identities and experiences and affirm their contribution to our art form and the communities we serve.

- **Equity:** OPERA America is committed to creating an equitable culture among its staff and board, and across all its programs. The organization will work with its members to implement fair policies and practices that create working environments free of prejudice, discrimination, and misogyny that respect and inspire all people equally. Equity means fairness for all, regardless of race, ethnicity, national origin, gender, sexual orientation, socio-economic status, religion, age, or disability status.

- **Inclusion:** Opera company leaders have begun to examine the attitudes, behaviors, and barriers that underlie the art form's exclusive traditions, while exploring ways to weave new connections into the mosaic of contemporary American life. As opera companies strive to establish mutually beneficial relationships with other arts and non-arts organizations in their communities, companies will introduce newcomers to the art form in a variety of settings and will welcome and value them as contributors to programming and organizational decision-making. Inclusion goes beyond numerical diversity to ensure authentic representation, empowered participation, and a true sense of belonging.

These definitions indicate that OPERA America has a fundamental understanding of the work needed in opera to address enduring racial ADEI issues. I also appreciate that they did not use one word, such as "cultural equity," "diversity," or "inclusion" as a catch-all for the work needed to achieve ADEI. As Sherbin and Rashid (2017) argued, diversity does not stick without inclusion. Furthermore, I believe specific strategies designed and framed to enhance and increase ADEI will work most effectively.

In my view, OPERA America's, *Commitment in Action* remains chief among its ADEI work thus far because the service arts organization holds itself accountable for institutionalizing the changes need to effectively manage their ADEI efforts and create seismic shifts across the opera industry. The statement reads as follows:

Through current programs and initiatives in development, OPERA America is committed to:

- Adoption of Equity Values and Practices: expand the commitment to equity, diversity, inclusion and gender parity as stated values and adopted practices, across the field.

- Diverse and Inclusive Boards and Staffs: increase diversity of its staff and Board of Directors and work with members to increase diversity on their staffs and boards, and among their audiences.
- Diverse and Inclusive Administrators: increase the recruitment, leadership development, and mentorship of women and people of color administrators.
- Diverse and Inclusive Casting and Hiring: work with members to understand and overcome biases and barriers to the commissioning and casting of people of color.
- Diverse and Inclusive Training: increase the recruitment, nurturing and retention of singers, conductors, directors and other artists, artisans and technicians of color, create similar opportunities for composers and librettists, and encourage the progress of administrators of color; and increase opportunities for women who are, or are aspiring to become, composers, librettists and company leaders, through grants and mentorship.
- Equity Training and Learning: with a focus on undoing racism and other biases, provide training and other learning resources on equity, diversity, and inclusivity to members through consultations, workshops, online resources and other means.

The remainder of the website included resources members can use to familiarize themselves with ADEI in opera, and throughout other areas of the cultural sector. Though OPERA America has done a great deal since 2018, the following four observations may strengthen their work, and help them to avoid some blindspots as they continue working to achieve ADEI in opera.

First, when it comes to ADEI, too many cultural organizations, including OPERA America, do not provide a cogent rationale that communicates why the sector needs ADEI. The rationale should explicitly articulate why OPERA America, or any cultural organization for that matter, has chosen to undertake ADEI work in the first place. Too many leaders who make the decision to move forward with ADEI work, rather than a training or equity assessment, assume that audiences, boards, communities, and staff know why ADEI work is important. This also happens in diversity trainings, which may explain why scholars have argued that trainings are largely ineffective, particularly as it relates to changing the behaviors of men and White people (Chang et al., 2019), two of the most privileged social identities in U.S. society and across the globe.

To address this particular challenge related to ADEI training, OPERA America and all cultural organizations should frame the impetus and need for ADEI as the result of discrimination, marginalization, and oppression throughout societies. In Table 8.4, I use Jackson and Griffin (2007) to show the different types of privileged and unprivileged social identities in U.S. society, and, to a degree, depending on cultural context, across the world. In these discussions and trainings, one must remind attendees that no one living today created this matrix of privilege and oppression. Even still, some benefit while others suffer as a result of maintaining this inherited system of privilege and oppression.

Second, by reviewing OPERA America's Equity, Diversity, and Inclusion page, I am not sure if the service arts organization conducted interviews or surveys to inform their process, or if the service arts organization simply has a deep understanding of the needs of the field and that informed their *Commitment in Action*. In a previous survey of the demographic diversity in the U.S. Arts Management workforce, I found that most arts managers identified as White, female, heterosexual, and abled-bodied. Also, about 14% of arts managers identified as LGBTQ+, which is higher than the national average of 5% (Cuyler, 2015). Although I requested access to data for this book, OPERA America did

Table 8.4 Matrix of oppression and privilege

Privileged social identities in the U.S.	Unprivileged social identities in the U.S.	Social oppression	Type of privilege
Temporarily abled-bodied people	Differently abled people	Ableism	Abled-bodied privilege
Owning class, upper middle class, middle class	Working-class or poor people	Classism	Class privilege
Heterosexuals	Bisexual, gay, lesbian, pansexual, and same-gender-loving individuals	Heterosexism	Heterosexual privilege
White people	Black, Indigenous, and people of color	Racism	White privilege
Christians	Agnostics, atheists, Buddhists, Hindi, Jews, Muslims, and other non-Christian religions	Religious oppression	Christian privilege
Cisgender men	Cisgender women, gender non-conforming people, transgender men, and women	Sexism	Male privilege

Note: Adapted from Jackson and Griffin (2007)

not share its demographic data on opera managers, if they collect it. Still, adopting a more evidence-based approach to addressing ADEI, similar to that practiced by the museum field (American Alliance of Museums, 2019; BoardSource, 2017; and Westermann, Schonfeld, & Sweeney, 2019), which included a survey of the demographic diversity of audiences, boards, and staff, will provide much-needed intel to develop better SMART goals and strategies to address racial ADEI issues in opera.

For example, OPERA America aspires to increase the recruitment, leadership development, and mentorship of women and administrators of color relative to diversity and inclusion. But, increase it from what to what? Using baseline data to inform their aspirations will ensure that OPERA America has meaningful progress to report in three to five years. Affirmative action-informed quotas or SMART goals have produced more success relative to access and diversity in U.S. society. Scholars (Cuyler, 2013; Kaplan, 2020; and Williams, 2017) highly encourage taking this approach because it moves away from the business case for diversity and moves in the direction of the ethical and legal case for ADEI. Furthermore, in the 21st century, OPERA America and its members need to adopt the mantra, "A White cisgender male, even if he identifies as gay, is not always the best candidate for the job."

Third, for its Opera Grants and Opera Residences grants program, OPERA America has adopted Inclusion, Diversity, Equity, and Access Success or the acronym IDEAS. I see potential issues with this. First, the messaging is not consistent with the Equity, Diversity, and Inclusivity page of OPERA America's website, which does not include a definition or discussion of Access in the definitions. Second, though I appreciate the cultural sector's ability to creatively develop acronyms such as IDEAS, some people may confuse the effort put into developing the acronym with the work. Lastly, IDEAS establishes a false premise about how the four frames work together to address discrimination, marginalization, and oppression, and the process by which this happens.

Therefore, I advocate for use of access, diversity, equity, and inclusion (ADEI), as I have used throughout this book, because an implicit procedure for how these frames work together exists. For example, all conversations and strategies must begin with access because throughout U.S. history people have been systematically and systemically excluded from fully participating in society based on specific social identities. Without the removal of barriers to participation, OPERA America will not achieve the extra and intra-group diversity needed to develop informed and meaningful strategies to achieve equity and inclusion. Elsewhere, I have also argued that the cultural sector should not pursue ADEI simply for the sake of achieving ADEI, but for the sake of achieving *creative justice*, which I define as the manifestation of all people living creative and expressive lives on their own terms (Cuyler, 2019).

Fourth, I emphatically support the idea of the African, LatinX, Asian, Arab, and Native American (ALAANA) Opera Network. But, what is the purpose of the network? How does the network inform OPERA America's ADEI efforts? Has OPERA America empowered the network to hold the service arts organization accountable for achieving the goals articulated in their *Commitment in Action*? Furthermore, how does one become a member of the network? When I clicked the link that invited me to join the network, it led me to Facebook. Since I do not have a Facebook account, does this mean that OPERA America will exclude me from joining the ALAANA Opera Network? To follow through on the seemingly comprehensive work done so far, OPERA America should think more deeply about all of the ways in which it can provide access to participation in this critical network to advance and support its ADEI work.

Similar to the ALAANA Opera Network, OPERA America has also facilitated an affinity network for women entitled, the Women's Opera Network (WON), which works to (1) increase awareness of and discussion about diversity and gender parity in the field, (2) create action plans to promote the advancement of talented women, (3) become a source of support for emerging female professionals. WON also has a mentorship program which aims to promote the advancement of women leaders in the field of opera administration. Based on its description and the evidence-based approach used to discuss the role of women in U.S. society and opera, I understand that WON is an older and more well-established affinity network. As is such, I am curious to see what gains the network has made since its founding. Nevertheless, WON gives me hope that OPERA America has the capacity to manage its ADEI efforts well and use a model that can inform the further development of the ALAANA Opera Network.

OPERA America has already begun to disseminate and implement aspects of their *Commitment to Action*. Of particular note are grant programs such as the IDEA Opera Grants, IDEA Opera Residencies, The Opera Fund: Civic Practice Grants, Opera Grants for Female Composers. Though I commend OPERA America for supporting advancement of the evolution of the art form through the telling of new stories in opera such as *Blind Injustice* (National Public Radio, 2019), *Blue* (Cartagena, 2019; Lunden, 2019), and *The Central Park Five* (Cooper, 2019), I strongly caution against monolithic portrayals of the lived experiences of people of color or other marginalized and oppressed groups as these stories can quickly turn into trauma porn. Though I planned to see *Blue* at the Kennedy Center in Washington, D.C. this year, I had to question my readiness to willingly expose myself to more content re-telling the trauma visited upon Black people through police brutality and racial violence. This viewing would have also come after attending a performance of Joel Thompson's *Seven Last Words of the Unarmed* last year and viewing the movie *Just Mercy*.

Balancing new operas with racially traumatic content with stories about exceptional historic individuals from marginalized and oppressed groups such as the opera, *Omar* (Parker, 2019), might make a good strategy. However, this, too, could unintentionally encourage audiences to stereotype marginalize and oppressed people as either victims or the canonical one. I strongly encourage OPERA America to use the grant programs to invite opera companies, and composers and librettist of color, to do what Torrie Allen suggested in his interview when he stated that, "Opera needs new stories, new ways of telling the classic stories, and the vitality and vibrancy that comes with greater variations of sensitivity and experience." The stories that companies choose to privilege through the profound art form of opera should maximize the potential of building bridges across cultures, and expand audiences' understandings of the human experience, which is rich and ripe for exploration.

The Finale

Opera education

In closing, I would like to give more attention to the question, "How might opera attract and retain more racially diverse managers?" Thinking more holistically about racial ADEI in opera, as Wayne Brown advocated, Williams and Graff's (2018) suggestion of building a lifelong love of opera through opera education heartens me. It should also encourage the opera industry to use education as an intervention to create multiple entry points into the art form for children and adults. Imagine, for example, an opera education program where adults served as "helpers." In this scenario, children take on active roles as board members, choreographers, composers, conductors, librettists, patrons, orchestra members, singers, stage directors, stage managers, and yes even opera managers. By simulating the roles the industry needs children to play when they become adults, opera will not only begin to prepare them well for these roles, but also strengthen the pipeline for future participation in opera. To continue asking children to take on passive roles as opera audiences when almost no empirical research exists to show that opera education in its current iteration helps to produce future opera audiences, board members, staff, or other key personnel needed is naïve and irresponsible.

African, LatinX, Asian, Arab, and Indigenous (ALAAI) opera companies

Since 1873, ALAAI opera companies have made remarkable contributions to diversifying opera audiences (Smith, 1994). However, the opera industry has all but ignored them instead of seeing them as critical partners. At times, some within the opera industry have expressed jealousy towards them. Linda Jackson described how a colleague expressed frustration at Opera North's ability to attract a large Black audience when Opera Philadelphia provided "better" productions. In addition, given the historic funding inequities implicitly imbedded in the cultural funding system (Helicon Collaborative, 2017; Sidford, 2011), ALAAI opera companies manage the challenges inherent in producing opera while also carrying the burden of the "other" within the industry. This leads me to wonder what possibilities might exist if OPERA America provided a grant program for ALAAI opera companies. How might such a program enrich and enhance the capacity of opera companies such as the Houston Ebony Opera, OperaCréole, Opera Cultura, Opera Noir, and Opera North, among others, to fulfill their missions and serve their audiences? In addition, what kinds of arts-based community engagement projects might emerge from a grant program that required legacy opera companies to partner with ALAAI opera companies?

ADEI consultants/professionals/scholars-in-residence

Seattle Opera serves as an innovative ADEI leader in opera. According to Bell (2018), Seattle Opera hired a Social Impact Consultant to help decolonize the art form and encourage more access to opera for communities of color. Furthermore, Seattle Opera engaged Dr. Naomi André as its inaugural scholar-in-residence (Alexander, 2020). Following Seattle Opera's lead, these two positions, or one position that features aspects of both positions, hold a great deal of promise for institutionalizing racial ADEI and creating seismic transformation across opera companies. For example, someone serving in a role of this nature might work with the board and staff on implicit bias. This is crucial work given that boards make critical hiring decisions in opera. If implicit racially biased groupthink unconsciously guides hiring decisions, it may explain why so few people of color receive executive-level jobs in opera. This strategy reinforces the idea that efforts made relative to access and diversity will not succeed without equity and inclusion. However, those who might consider this strategy must keep in mind that diversity and implicit bias training are not a silver bullet. Indeed, these types of trainings have done little to change the behaviors of men and White people (Chang et al., 2019). The best thing about this idea is that the Mellon Foundation, among others, have demonstrated interest in funding this kind of work.

Fellowship and mentorship

Although every executive opera manager of color in this book acknowledged receiving critical mentorship along their career paths, a glaring lack of mentorship on most of their part emerged as a major stumbling block to achieving racial ADEI in opera. To address the access and diversity aspects of the work, a paid fellowship program, similar to the one OPERA America had for years, which explicitly recruits and seeks to retain people of color in opera management, could make significant impacts.

In addition to recruiting aspiring opera managers of color, the program should target those who aspire to pursue executive-level positions. In addition to a robust professional development program, OPERA America should also consider how it might engage the executive opera managers of color profiled in this book in the mentorship of the next generation of opera managers of color. The program should also include cross-cultural mentorship because it clearly made a huge difference in the careers of the executive opera managers of color profiled in this book.

With a great deal of caution, I advise that those who might manage all aspects of the fellowship including career coaching, mentorship, and programming should undergo in-depth cultural sensitivity training. As an external evaluator of a similar program, I have observed program managers undermine their efforts and intentions with unintended cultural hubris, incompetence, and insensitivity including dismissing and minimizing the professional experience and expertise of the very people the program aimed to serve. Creating these kinds of opportunities for people of color would also identify aspiring opera managers of color who have had difficulty navigating careers in the sector (Stein, 2000).

In closing, I invite the opera industry to consider framing its ADEI work through the lens of what Banks (2017) called *creative justice*. I defined *creative justice* as the manifestation of all people living creative lives on their own terms (Cuyler, 2019). What would it mean for the U.S. and global opera industry if *creative justice* underpinned every artistic, managerial, and personnel decision? What might happen if the opera industry actively sought to use opera as an intervention to ensure and promote *creative justice* for all people? Lastly, who and what opportunities will the opera industry continue to miss out on engaging with by not adopting *creative justice* as the defining motivation and rationale for all of its ADEI work? With answers to these questions, I remain hopeful that the opera industry can envision a path forward where all can experience the transformative magnificence of opera.

References

Alexander, G. (2020). Seattle Opera may have the country's only opera scholar in residence, helping make the art form more diverse and relevant. *The Seattle Times*. Accessed May 28, 2020. www.seattletimes.com/entertainment/classical-music/seattle-opera-may-have-the-countrys-only-opera-scholar-in-residence-helping-make-the-art-form-more-diverse-and-relevant/?mc_cid=0b829fc4c9& mc_eid=4254e9122a.

American Alliance of Museums. (2019). *Facing change: Insights from the American Alliance of Museums' Diversity, Equity, Accessibility, and Inclusion Working Group*. Accessed December 13, 2019. www.aam-us.org/wp-content/ uploads/2018/04/AAM-DEAI-Working-Group-Full-Report-2018.pdf.

Banks, M. (2017). *Creative justice: Cultural industries, work, and inequality*. Rowman & Littlefield.

Bell, C. (2018). Seattle opera checks its privilege. *Crosscut*. Accessed December 13, 2019. https://crosscut.com/2018/04/seattle-opera-checks-its-privilege.

Bivens, D. K. (2005). *What is internalized racism?* In M. Potapchuk, S. Leiderman, D. Bivens, & B. Major (Eds.), *Flipping the script: White privilege and community building* (p. 44). Accessed December 13, 2019. www.racialequity tools.org/resourcefiles/What_is_Internalized_Racism.pdf.

BoardSource. (2017). *Museum board leadership: A national report*. Accessed December 13, 2019. www.aam-us.org/wp-content/uploads/2018/01/eyizzp-download-the-report.pdf.

Cartagena, R. (2019). *Why the Kennedy Center is developing an opera about police brutality*. Accessed December 13, 2019. www.washingtonian.com/2019/ 04/03/kennedy-center-opera-blue-police-brutality/.

Chang, E. H., Milkman, K. L., Zarrow, L. J., Brabaw, K., Gromet, D. M., Rebele, R., Massey, C., Duckworth, A. L., & Grant, A. (2019). Does diversity training work the way it's supposed to? *Harvard Business Review*. Accessed December 13, 2019. https://hbr.org/2019/07/does-diversity-training-work-the-way-its-supposed-to.

Cooper, M. (2019). This summer, opera grapples with race. *The New York Times*. Accessed December 13, 2019. www.nytimes.com/2019/05/30/arts/music/central-park-five-opera.html.

Crenshaw, K. (1989). Demarginalizing the intersection of race and sex: A Black feminist critique of antidiscrimination doctrine, feminist theory and antiracist politics. *University of Chicago Legal Forum*, 1989(1), 139–167.

Cuyler, A. C. (2019). The role of foundations in achieving creative justice. *GIA Reader*, 30(1), 57–62.

Cuyler, A. C. (2015). An exploratory study of demographic diversity in the arts management workforce. *GIA Reader*, 26(3), 16–19.

Cuyler, A. C. (2013). Affirmative action and diversity: Implication for Arts Management. *Journal of Arts Management, Law, and Society*, 43(2), 98–105.

Helicon Collaborative. (2017). *Not just money: Equity issues in cultural philanthropy*. Accessed December 13, 2019. https://heliconcollab.net/our_work/not-just-money/.

Jackson, B., & Griffin, P. (2007). Conceptual foundations for social justice education. In M. Adams, L. Bell, & P. Griffin (Eds.), *Teaching for diversity and social justice* (2nd ed., p. 42). Routledge.

Kaplan, S. (2020). Why the 'business case' for diversity isn't working. *Fast Company*. Accessed 28 May, 2020. www.fastcompany.com/90462867/why-the-business-case-for-diversity-isnt-working?mc_cid=d276106cf3&mc_eid=4254e9122a.

Lunden, J. (2019). New opera 'Blue' takes on the tragedy of police brutality. *NPR*. Accessed December 13, 2019. www.npr.org/2019/07/21/743206920/new-opera-blue-takes-on-the-tragedy-of-police-brutality.

Marrow, J. (2018). What we're learning about Nonprofits' DEI journeys. *GuideStar Blog*. Accessed December 13, 2019. Accessed December 13, 2019. https://trust.guidestar.org/what-were-learning-about-nonprofits-dei-journeys?utm_campaign=GuideStar%20Newsletter%20-%20Nonprofits&utm_source=hs_email&utm_medium=email&utm_content=64214164&_hsenc=p2ANqtz-96YRh-_Z6EISCjYra-Fwe4H0keEOGwQMOjVgLag6zwtJ09GItnzz-0tKwnJG2irjHrp1rr soOtgqoZqTdFZuTQEZ_oKg&_hsmi=64226988.

National Public Radio. (2019). 'Blind Injustice' opera sets out to open eyes about wrongful conviction rates. *NPR*. Accessed December 13, 2019. www.ijpr.org/post/blind-injustice-opera-sets-out-open-eyes-about-wrongful-conviction-rates#stream/0.

OPERA America. (2020). *OPERA America's commitment to Equity, Diversity and Inclusivity (EDI) values*. Accessed May 28, 2020. www.operaamerica.org/content/about/EDI/index.aspx.

National Endowment for the Arts (1965). *Annual report 1964–1965*. Accessed May 28, 2020. www.arts.gov/sites/default/files/NEA-Annual-Report-1964-1965.pdf.

Parker, A. (2019). Spoleto to stage opera in 2020 featuring real-life story of a Muslim slave in Charleston. *The Post and Courier*. Accessed December 13, 2019. www.postandcourier.com/spoleto/spoleto-to-stage-opera-in-featuring-real-life-story-of/article_2e0c7006-89fd-11e9-b5f2-5fec51f51b78.html.

Sherbin, L., & Rashid, R. (2017). Diversity doesn't stick without inclusion. *The Harvard Business Review*. Accessed December 13, 2019. https://hbr.org/2017/02/diversity-doesnt-stick-without-inclusion?utm_campaign=hbr&utm_source=linkedin&utm_medium=social.

Sidford, H. (2011). *Fusing arts, culture and social change: High impact strategies for philanthropy*. Accessed December 13, 2019. http://heliconcollab.net/wp-content/uploads/2013/04/Fusing-Arts_Culture_and_Social_Change1.pdf.

Smith, E. L. (1994). *Blacks in opera: An encyclopedia of people and companies, 1873–1993*. McFarland Press.

Stein, T. S. (2000). Creating opportunities for people of color in performing arts management. *Journal of Arts Management, Law, and Society*, 29(4), 304–318.

Westermann, M., Schonfeld, R., & Sweeney, L. (2019). *Art museum staff demographic survey 2018*. Accessed December 13, 2019. https://mellon.org/media/filer_public/b1/21/b1211ce7-5478-4a06-92df-3c88fa472446/sr-mellon-report-art-museum-staff-demographic-survey-01282019.pdf.

Williams, H., & Graff, P. (2018). Building a lifelong love of opera in toddlers, one hop at a time. *Reuters*. Accessed December 13, 2019. www.reuters.com/article/us-britain-opera-toddlers/building-a-lifelong-love-of-opera-in-toddlers-one-hop-at-a-time-idUSKCN1MR079?mc_cid=d32ea26a55&mc_eid=4254e9122a.

Williams, J. B. (2017). Breaking down bias: Legal mandates vs. corporate interests. *Georgetown Law Faculty Publications and Other Works*. Accessed December 13, 2019. https://scholarship.law.georgetown.edu/facpub/1961/.

Index

Note: Information in tables is indicated by **bold** page numbers.

Printed in the United States
by Baker & Taylor Publisher Services